THE
TRUTH

ENGAGING THE FOUNDATIONS
OF THE FAITH

LifeWay Press®
Nashville, Tennessee

⬚ DISCIPLES PATH

Disciples Path is a series of studies founded on Jesus' model of discipleship. Created by experienced disciple makers across the nation, it offers an intentional pathway for transformational discipleship and a way to help followers of Christ move from new disciples to mature disciple makers. Each study in the series is built on the principles of modeling, practicing, and multiplying:

- Leaders model the life of a biblical disciple.

- Disciples follow and practice from the leader.

- Disciples become disciple makers and multiply through the *Disciples Path*.

Each study in the series has been written and approved by disciple makers for small groups and one-on-one settings.

Contributors:

Dr. Craig Etheredge; First Baptist Church; Colleyville, Texas

Josh Howerton; The Bridge Church; Spring Hill, Tennessee

MINISTRY GRID
training made simple

For helps on how to use *Disciples Path,* tips on how to better lead groups, or additional ideas for leading this study, visit: *ministrygrid.com/web/disciplespath*

Item 005717353 • ISBN 978-1-4300-3953-2
Dewey decimal classification: 248.84
Subject headings: DISCIPLESHIP \ JESUS CHRIST \ CHRISTIAN LIFE

Eric Geiger
Vice President, LifeWay Resources

Rick Howerton
Discipleship Specialist

Sam O'Neal, Joel Polk
Content Editors

Brian Daniel
Manager, Discipleship Publishing

Michael Kelley
Director, Groups Ministry

We believe that the Bible has God for its author; salvation for its end; and truth, without any mixture of error, for its matter and that all Scripture is totally true and trustworthy. To review LifeWay's doctrinal guideline, visit *www.lifeway.com/doctrinalguideline.*

Unless otherwise noted, all Scripture quotations are taken from the Holman Christian Standard Bible®, copyright 1999, 2000, 2002, 2003, 2009 by Holman Bible Publishers. Used by permission. Scripture marked NIV is taken from the NEW INTERNATIONAL VERSION®. Copyright © 1973, 1978, 1984 by Biblica Inc. All rights reserved worldwide. Used by permission. Scripture quotations marked NLT are taken from the Holy Bible, New Living Translation, copyright © 1996, 2004, 2007 by Tyndale House Foundation. Used by permission of Tyndale House Publishers Inc., Carol Stream, Illinois 60188. All rights reserved. Scripture marked NASB is taken from the NEW AMERICAN STANDARD BIBLE®, Copyright © 1960,1962,1963, 1968,1 971,1972,1973,1975,1977,1995 by The Lockman Foundation. Used by permission. Scripture quotations marked ESV are taken from The Holy Bible, English Standard Version® (ESV®), copyright © 2001 by Crossway, a publishing ministry of Good News Publishers. Used by permission. All rights reserved.

To order additional copies of this resource, write to LifeWay Resources Customer Service; One LifeWay Plaza; Nashville, TN 37234-0113; fax 615.251.5933; call toll free 800.458.2772; order online at *www.lifeway.com;* email *orderentry@lifeway.com;* or visit the LifeWay Christian Store serving you.

Printed in the United States of America

Groups Ministry Publishing • LifeWay Resources
One LifeWay Plaza • Nashville, TN 37234-0152

CONTENTS

A NOTE FOR DISCIPLE MAKERS

Several years ago I was part of a massive research study that sought to discover how the Lord often brings about transformation in the hearts of His people. The study became a book called *Transformational Discipleship*. Basically, we wanted to learn how disciples are made. Based on the study of Scripture and lots of interactions with people, we concluded that transformation is likely to occur when a godly **leader** applies **truth** to the heart of a person while that person is in a teachable **posture.**

- **LEADER:** You are the leader. As you invest in the people you're discipling, they will learn much about the Christian faith by watching you, by sensing your heart for the Lord, and by seeing you pursue Him. I encourage you to seek to be the type of leader who can say, "Follow my example as I follow the example of Christ."

- **TRUTH:** All six studies in the *Disciples Path* series were developed in deep collaboration with ministry leaders who regularly and effectively disciple people. The studies are designed to take the people you disciple into the Word of God—because we're confident that Jesus and His Word sanctify us and transform us. Our community of disciple-makers mapped out a path of the truths we believe are essential for each believer to know and understand.

- **POSTURE:** Hopefully the people you will be investing in adopt a teachable posture—one that is open and hungry for the Lord. Encourage them to take the study seriously and to view your invitation to study together as a sacred opportunity to experience the grace of God and the truth of God.

We hope and pray the Lord will use this study in your life and the lives of those you disciple. As you apply the truth of God to teachable hearts, transformation will occur. Thank you for being a disciple-maker!

In Christ,

Eric Geiger
Vice President at LifeWay Christian Resources
Co-author of *Transformational Discipleship*

WHAT IS A DISCIPLE?

Congratulations! If you've chosen to live as a disciple of Jesus, you've made the most important decision imaginable. But you may be wondering, *What does it mean to be a disciple?*

To put it simply, a disciple of Jesus is someone who has chosen to follow Jesus. That's the command Jesus gave to those He recruited as His first disciples: "Follow Me." In Jesus' culture, religious leaders called rabbis would gather a group of followers called disciples to follow in their footsteps and learn their teachings. In the same way, you will become more and more like Jesus as you purposefully follow Him in the weeks to come. Jesus once said, "Everyone who is fully trained will be like his teacher" (Luke 6:40).

On a deeper level, disciples of Jesus are those learning to base their identities on Jesus Himself. All of us use different labels to describe who we are at the core levels of our hearts. Some think of themselves as athletes or intellectuals. Others think of themselves as professionals, parents, leaders, class clowns, and so on.

Disciples of Jesus set aside those labels and base their identities on Him. For example:

- **A disciple of Jesus is a child of God.** In the Bible we find these words: "Look at how great a love the Father has given us that we should be called God's children. And we are!" (1 John 3:1). We are God's children. He loves us as our perfect Father.

- **A disciple of Jesus is an alien in this world.** Disciples of Jesus are aliens, or outsiders, in their own cultures. Because of this identity, Jesus' disciples abstain from actions and activities that are contrary to Him. Peter, one of Jesus' original disciples, wrote these words: "Dear friends, I urge you as strangers and temporary residents to abstain from fleshly desires that war against you" (1 Pet. 2:11).

- **A disciple of Jesus is an ambassador for Christ.** Another of Jesus' disciples recorded these words in the Bible: "Therefore, if anyone is in Christ, he is a new creation; old things have passed away, and look, new things have come. ... Therefore, we are ambassadors for Christ, certain that God is appealing through us. We plead on Christ's behalf, 'Be reconciled to God'" (2 Cor. 5:17,20). Ambassadors represent their king and country in a different culture for a specified period of time. Because we have been transformed by Jesus and are now His disciples and ambassadors, we represent Him to the world through our actions and by telling others about Him.

The journey you are about to take is one that will transform you more and more to be like Jesus. Enjoy! No one ever loved and cared for people more passionately than Jesus. No one was ever more sincere in His concern for others than Jesus. And no one ever gave more so that we could experience His love than Jesus did on the cross.

As you grow to be more like Jesus, you'll find that your relationships are stronger, you have more inner peace than ever before, and you look forward to the future as never before.

That's the blessing of living as a disciple of Jesus.

HOW TO USE THIS RESOURCE

Welcome to *The Truth*. By exploring the journey of Jesus' earliest disciples, both new and established Christians will gain a better understanding of what it means to follow Christ. As you get started, consider the following guides and suggestions for making the most of this experience.

GROUP DISCUSSION

Because the process of discipleship always involves at least two people—the leader and the disciple—each session of *The Truth* includes a practical plan for group engagement and discussion.

This plan includes the following steps:

- **GET STARTED.** The first section of the group material helps you ease into the discussion by starting on common ground. You'll begin by reflecting on the previous session and your recent experiences as a disciple. After spending time in prayer, you'll find a practical illustration to help you launch into the main topic of the current session.

- **THE STORY.** While using *Disciples Path*, you'll find opportunities to engage the Bible through both story and teaching. That's why the group time for each session features two main sections: **Know the Story** and **Unpack the Story. Know the Story** introduces a biblical text and includes follow-up questions for brief discussion. It's recommended that your group encounter the biblical text by reading it out loud. **Unpack the Story** includes practical teaching material and discussion questions—both designed to help you engage the truths contained in the biblical text. To make the most of your experience, use the provided material as a launching point for deeper conversation. As you read through the teaching material and engage the questions as a group, be thinking of how the truths you're exploring will impact your everyday life.

- **ENGAGE.** The group portion of each session ends with an activity designed to help you practice the biblical principles introduced in **Know the Story** and more fully explored in **Unpack the Story.** This part of the group time often appeals to different learning styles and will push you to engage the text at a personal level.

INDIVIDUAL DISCOVERY

Each session of *The Truth* also includes content for individual use during the time between group gatherings. This content is divided into three categories:

⬆ **Worship:** features content for worship and devotion. These activities provide opportunities for you to connect with God in meaningful ways and deepen your relationship with Him.

➡⬅ **Personal study:** features content for personal study. These pages help you gain a deeper understanding of the truths and principles explored during the group discussion.

⬅➡ **Application:** features content for practical application. These suggestions help you take action based on the information you've learned and your encounters with God.

Note: Aside from the **Reading Plan,** the content provided in the Individual Discovery portion of each session should be considered optional. You'll get the most out of your personal study by working with your group leader to create a personalized discipleship plan using the **Weekly Activities** checklist included in each session.

ADDITIONAL SUGGESTIONS

- You'll be best prepared for each group discussion or mentoring conversation if you read the session material beforehand. A serious read will serve you most effectively, but skimming the **Get Started** and **The Story** sections will also be helpful if time is limited.

- The deeper you're willing to engage in the group discussions and individual discovery each session, the more you'll benefit from those experiences. Don't hold back, and don't be afraid to ask questions whenever necessary.

- As you explore the **Engage** portion of each session, you'll have the chance to practice different activities and spiritual disciplines. Take advantage of the chance to observe others during the group time—and to ask questions—so that you'll be prepared to incorporate these activities into your private spiritual life as well.

- Visit *lifeway.com/disciplespath* for a free PDF download that includes leader helps for *The Truth* and additional resources for disciple-makers.

THE DOCTRINE OF GOD

God is the Triune Creator on
mission to redeem the world

REFLECT

Welcome to *The Truth*. The goal of this resource is to help you engage and understand the basic doctrines—the core beliefs and principles—of the Christian faith. Throughout the following sessions, we'll examine what the Bible teaches on key issues such as God, humanity, the Person and work of Jesus, the kingdom of God, the Holy Spirit, and the church.

Use the following questions to begin the session with discussion.

How confident do you feel in your knowledge of Christian doctrine?

What are you hoping to learn or experience during this study?

When did you begin to think seriously about God and His role in the universe?

PRAY

Begin the session by connecting with God through prayer. Use the following guidelines as you speak with Him:

- Thank God for the opportunity to join with other disciples of Jesus in order to explore the critical doctrines expressed in His Word.

- Praise God for the wisdom and truth expressed in every page of the Bible.

- Ask for wisdom and understanding as you seek to gain a deeper understanding of God's character and role in the world.

INTRODUCTION

A. W. Tozer once wrote, "What comes into our minds when we think about God is the most important thing about us."[1] That is certainly true. God is the Creator and Sustainer of all things; therefore, we cannot be anything or accomplish anything that transcends our connection with Him.

Still, it's important in a study like this one to remember that *thinking* about God is only the beginning. Believing information about God with our heads is only one part of forming a relationship with Him. We must also develop that relationship through our hearts—through our emotions and affections.

In this way, our relationship with God should resemble the sun, which produces both *light* and *heat*. Take a moment to think about our solar system. If the sun produced nothing but light, our planet would be an illuminated wasteland of solid ice. If the sun produced nothing but heat, the lovely diversity of our world would be shrouded in darkness. Only the combination of light and heat produces life.

Those who embrace an intellectual understanding of God may have proper doctrine. However, beliefs won't do us any good if they fail to push us toward an actual love and appreciation of our Creator. Similarly, today's culture is filled with people who demonstrate a genuine passion for spiritual principles and ideas, yet direct that passion toward false idols or false ideas about God. Both approaches are ultimately unfulfilling.

What are the practical consequences of focusing too much on the intellectual side of following God?

What are the practical consequences of focusing too much on our emotions and passion?

As we'll see in this session, God has revealed Himself as the Triune Creator—three separate Persons who make up one Being—who is on a mission to redeem the world. That's a critical doctrine that all disciples of Jesus need to understand. Yet even as you engage the light of the Scriptures throughout this study, don't forget to allow the warmth of God's love to penetrate your own heart. Both are necessary.

KNOW THE STORY

The first words in the Bible are, "In the beginning" (Gen. 1:1). Looking at verse 1 in the Scripture below, it's clear that John wanted to make a bold statement at the beginning of his Gospel. In many ways, John 1 serves as a restatement of Genesis 1.

Not surprisingly, these verses can teach us a great deal about the character of God.

¹ In the beginning was the Word,
and the Word was with God,
and the Word was God.
² He was with God in the beginning.
³ All things were created through Him,
and apart from Him not one thing was created
that has been created.
⁴ Life was in Him,
and that life was the light of men. ...
¹¹ He came to His own,
and His own people did not receive Him.
¹² But to all who did receive Him,
He gave them the right to be children of God,
to those who believe in His name,
¹³ who were born,
not of blood,
or of the will of the flesh,
or of the will of man,
but of God.
¹⁴ The Word became flesh
and took up residence among us.
We observed His glory,
the glory as the One and Only Son from the Father,
full of grace and truth.
JOHN 1:1-4,11-14

What do these verses teach us about God?

UNPACK THE STORY

GOD IS THE TRIUNE CREATOR

In the very first verse of his Gospel, the apostle John made a crucial declaration that's easy to miss if you're not looking for it. Here it is:

> In the beginning was the Word,
> and the Word was with God,
> and the Word was God.
> **JOHN 1:1**

When John wrote about "the Word," he was actually talking about Jesus. That's why verse 14 says "the Word became flesh and took up residence among us." So, the crucial declaration John made in verse 1 is that Jesus is God. According to this Gospel, Jesus and God are the same Being.

If we believe God to be infinite and all-powerful, we should never expect to condense Him into a formula we can understand.

All of this points to a foundational aspect of God's nature: He is the Trinity. The Father, the Son (Jesus), and the Holy Spirit are all one God. Together they form the Deity who created everything out of nothing. Put another way, you can describe God as one "what" and three "who's." He is one Essence, one Being, who exists in three Persons. So, if someone asks you whether God is one or three, the best response is, "Yes."

What, if anything, have you been taught about the nature of the Trinity?

What questions would you like to ask about the Trinity?

The doctrine of the Trinity is something theologians have historically called an incommunicable aspect of God. Meaning, it's something that human beings cannot grasp. This shouldn't surprise us or even insult us. After all, if we believe God to be infinite and all-powerful, we should never expect to condense Him into a formula we can understand.

How do you respond to the concept of an "incommunicable aspect of God"?

GOD HAS A MISSION TO REDEEM THE WORLD

While it's a challenge to contemplate God's nature as three Persons interconnected within a single Being, we have an easier time identifying God's motives when it comes to us and our world. All we have to do is follow the verbs. For example, when we look at the verbs in Genesis 1, it's clear that God was focused on creating the different elements of our world:

- "Then God said, 'Let there be light,' and there was light" (v. 3).
- "So God created the large sea-creatures and every living creature that moves and swarms in the water, according to their kinds" (v. 21).
- "Then God said, 'Let Us make man in Our image, according to Our likeness'" (v. 26).

What about John 1? If this chapter was constructed as a restatement of Genesis 1, what did the apostle John want to communicate about God's mission and motives?

Read through John 1:11-14 again. What do these verses teach us about God's mission and motives?

One of the main messages of the Bible is that God's creative work in Genesis 1 was eventually corrupted by the presence of human sinfulness. What God created as "good" and "very good" became broken and stained. It makes sense, then, that John's Gospel begins with God's heart to redeem and repair the damage of our sin.

The verbs are fascinating: "He *came* to His own" (v. 11). "He *gave* them the right to be children of God" (v. 12). "The Word *became* flesh" (v. 14). Each of these terms shines a spotlight on God's mission to redeem the world and offer salvation to all people. The verbs reveal an active mission, as well. God didn't remain distant and arrange for our salvation from heaven. He jumped into our world to rescue it and us.

God didn't remain distant and arrange for our salvation from heaven. He jumped into our world to rescue it and us.

How would you describe your first encounters with God?

As you work through this study, remember that mission and salvation are not simply things God does; they are a part of who He is. God delighted in saving you because He loves you, that's true. But also God is a Savior at His core—so much that He willingly sacrificed Himself for us.

ENGAGE

As disciples of Jesus, evangelism is one of the duties to which we've been called. We have a responsibility to proclaim the message of the gospel within our spheres of influence—to help people understand who God is and what He has done.

Unfortunately, we can't "explain" God in the same way we can explain a math problem or the best way to bake an apple pie. He is God! What we can do, however, is help people understand the basic elements of God's nature and character—and then work to help them experience Him for themselves.

With that in mind, the image below offers a starting point for helping others to begin thinking through the doctrine of the Trinity. Work as a group to practice drawing out the image. Also practice explaining the basic idea of the Trinity to one another so that you'll be ready to help others who want to gain a better understanding of who God is and what He has done.

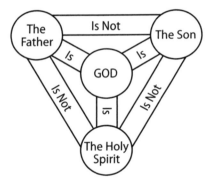

PRAYER REQUESTS

....

....

....

....

....

....

....

....

1. A. W. Tozer, *The Knowledge of the Holy* (New York: HarperCollins, 1961), 1.

In addition to studying God's Word, work with your group leader to create a plan for personal study, worship, and application between now and the next session. Select from the following optional activities to match your personal preferences and available time.

↑ Worship

☑ Read your Bible. Complete the reading plan on page 16.

☐ Spend time with God by engaging the devotional experience on page 17.

☐ Connect with God each day through prayer.

➡ ⬅ Personal Study

☐ Read and interact with "God Is the Triune Creator" on page 18.

☐ Read and interact with "God Has a Mission to Redeem the World" on page 20.

⬅ ➡ Application

☐ Take some time to study God's Word and worship Him in a natural setting. Consider what you can learn about God from the world He created.

☐ Memorize Isaiah 40:28: "Do you not know? Have you not heard? Yahweh is the everlasting God, the Creator of the whole earth. He never grows faint or weary; there is no limit to His understanding."

☐ Make an intentional effort to draw and explain the Trinity chart (see p. 14) for someone before the next session.

☐ Start a journal to record your reflections on the different doctrines you'll explore throughout this study. Commit to thinking about what you learn from each session, and then record your questions and insights for later discussion.

☐ Other:

 # WORSHIP

READING PLAN

Read through the following Scripture passages this week. Use the space provided to record your thoughts and responses.

Day 1
Genesis 1:1-31

Day 2
Exodus 33:12–34:9

Day 3
Jeremiah 10:1-16

Day 4
John 16:12-33

Day 5
Romans 1:18-32

Day 6
Hebrews 8:1-13

Day 7
Revelation 4:1-11

DIVINE TESTIMONY

There's no greater authority on who God is than God Himself. That's why God's Word is the best place to find information about God's nature and character. In the following passage, for example, God takes the incredible step of revealing a piece of Himself to Moses after the exodus from Egypt:

> [5] The LORD came down in a cloud, stood with him there, and proclaimed His name Yahweh. [6] Then the LORD passed in front of him and proclaimed: Yahweh—Yahweh is a compassionate and gracious God, slow to anger and rich in faithful love and truth, [7] maintaining faithful love to a thousand generations, forgiving wrongdoing, rebellion, and sin. But He will not leave the guilty unpunished, bringing the consequences of the fathers' wrongdoing on the children and grandchildren to the third and fourth generation.
> **EXODUS 34:5-7**

Use the following questions to help you reflect on this passage.

What do these verses teach you about God?

How have you recently experienced one of God's characteristics described in these verses?

What aspect of God's character would you like to experience more fully in your life?

Of course, the best way to learn about God is to experience Him through real and personal encounters. Spend several minutes in prayer. Proclaim your desire to know more about Him and to experience Him in a meaningful way. Then be silent. Allow yourself to listen for the voice of His Spirit and feel the reality of His presence with you.

GOD IS THE TRIUNE CREATOR

One of the interesting aspects of studying the Trinity in Scripture is that you'll never find the word *Trinity* in Scripture—not even in the original Hebrew or Greek languages. Indeed, *Trinity* is a term that Bible scholars created in order to discuss God's existence as three distinct Persons united in a single Being.

However, that doesn't mean the concept of the Trinity is foreign or the Scriptures are outside the boundaries of biblical doctrine. In fact, the presence of the Trinity can be felt throughout the entirety of God's Word—starting with the beginning:

> ¹ In the beginning God created the heavens and the earth. ² Now the earth was formless and empty, darkness covered the surface of the watery depths, and the Spirit of God was hovering over the surface of the waters. ³ Then God said, "Let there be light," and there was light.
> **GENESIS 1:1-3**

The very first verses of the Bible make direct references to God the Father and God the Holy Spirit. But Jesus is there, too, if you know where to look. Remember what John wrote in the first verses of his Gospel:

> ¹ In the beginning was the Word,
> and the Word was with God,
> and the Word was God.
> ² He was with God in the beginning.
> ³ All things were created through Him,
> and apart from Him not one thing was created
> that has been created.
> **JOHN 1:1-3**

How do these verses influence your understanding of Genesis 1:1-3?

Because we are created in God's image (see Gen. 1:26-27), what does the nature of the Trinity say about us?

Perhaps the clearest representation of the Trinity occurred during Jesus' baptism at the very beginning of His public ministry:

> [16] After Jesus was baptized, He went up immediately from the water. The heavens suddenly opened for Him, and He saw the Spirit of God descending like a dove and coming down on Him. [17] And there came a voice from heaven:
>
> This is My beloved Son.
> I take delight in Him!
> **MATTHEW 3:16-17**

Again, it's difficult for us to fully process what is happening in these verses. On the one hand, we can see three distinct persons acting in different ways—Jesus was baptized as a human being, the Holy Spirit descended from above in the form of a dove, and God the Father spoke an audible pronouncement of His pleasure with Jesus. At the same time, we know that all three of those Persons exist as one Being. All three are God at the same time.

That's the mystery of the Trinity.

Read the following passages of Scripture and record how they contribute to your understanding of the Trinity.

Matthew 28:18-20

John 14:23-26

2 Corinthians 13:11-13

PERSONAL STUDY 2

GOD HAS A MISSION TO REDEEM THE WORLD

When we think about the doctrine of God, we are really attempting to address two major questions: What is God like? What does God do?

How would you answer these questions right now?

The short answer to the first question is: "the Trinity." As we've seen, it's understandably difficult for human beings to process the nature and character of God. The best way we can describe what He is like is three distinct Persons living in perfect community as a single Being. That's the Trinity.

The short answer to the second question is: "everything." God created everything in the universe, and He is solely responsible for sustaining everything He created. God is both the source of all things and the ultimate purpose for all things. And that's only a part of what He does. It's also true that, since God exists as a perfect community, another part of what He does is enjoy a relationship with Himself—and with everything He has created.

The Bible helps us understand these big-picture concepts, but that's not its primary focus. Instead, the Scriptures are mainly focused on one specific aspect of what God does. Namely, they help us see God's long-term mission to redeem His creation—including both the world He created and the people He loves.

As you discussed earlier in this session, God's original creation was corrupted by human sin. In response, God initiated a long-term plan designed to re-establish a connection between Himself and humanity—a plan that culminated in Jesus Christ. John offered a helpful summary of that moment:

> The Word became flesh
> and took up residence among us.
> We observed His glory,
> the glory as the One and Only Son from the Father,
> full of grace and truth.
> **JOHN 1:14**

Read the following passages of Scripture and record what they teach about God's mission to redeem the world:

Genesis 12:1-3

Leviticus 26:3-17

Jeremiah 31:31-34

Matthew 28:16-20

Revelation 21:1-8

The total message of the Bible makes it clear that God has personally involved Himself in the mission to restore His creation. He's not a "divine Watchmaker" who created the universe only to remain distant from whatever happens within it. He's not an angry Creator waiting on the edge of His seat to destroy us for our disobedience.

Instead, God has lovingly and patiently worked with us and extended Himself toward us in order to redeem us and restore our relationship with Him.

What are some ways God's mission is evident today?

THE DOCTRINE OF HUMANITY

Human dignity has been distorted by depravity.

REFLECT

In the previous session we looked at the doctrine of God. We saw that God is the Triune Creator—that He exists as one Being in three Persons. We also saw that God has a mission to redeem our broken world. This is consistent with His character because redemption isn't just something God does; it's a major part of who He is. He is a Savior.

As you prepare to explore the doctrine of humanity, take a moment to reflect on your experiences in recent days.

Which of the assignments did you explore this week? How did it go?

What did you learn or experience while reading the Bible?

What questions would you like to ask?

PRAY

Take a break from your discussion and approach God together in prayer. Use the following guidelines as you connect with Him:

- Praise God for the character trait that stood out to you.

- Ask God to speak to you through this session and reveal a new truth to you from His Word.

- Pray that God would soften your heart and allow you to hear from Him regarding your need for a Savior.

INTRODUCTION

Imagine you're sitting down at a potter's wheel. You scoop the raw, gray clay out of the worn bucket beside you. Slowly, you begin to pour water on the clay as you manipulate the pedals at your feet to start turning the wheel. As the blob of clay begins to spin, you use your hands to shape the clay. Clumpy, hard parts begin to smooth out as you apply just the right amount of pressure. As you cut off the excess material, your lump of clay starts to resemble a small jar.

Your eyes are focused. Your hands are steady. The vision in your mind is becoming reality.

As you're working at the wheel, maybe you envision a day when this jar will be painted and used in your kitchen. Or maybe you dream of giving this handmade pottery to a friend as a gift. There are so many uses for this clump of clay.

But then something goes wrong. The clay collapses, the image is distorted, and the dream of using this clay for its purpose dies. What will you do? Will you scrap the clay altogether and start over with a new batch? Maybe you can remake the clay into something else. Maybe the clay is still valuable and useful.

This was the image the prophet Jeremiah saw when he visited a potter's house. The master craftsman was at the wheel, working deliberately, intentionally, and patiently. But then the clay was marred; the design was ruined in his hands. Yet the potter didn't scrap the clay. Instead he reshaped it into something beautiful. Then Jeremiah heard these words: " 'Can I not treat you as this potter treats his clay?'—this is the LORD'S declaration. 'Just like clay in the potter's hand, so are you in My hand, house of Israel' " (Jer. 18:6).

Read Jeremiah 18:1-12. How does the story of the potter's wheel reflect our relationship with God?

What circumstances or modern realities best illustrate how God's creation has been marred by sin?

Let's continue exploring God's interaction with His prize creations—human beings—as we move into the key text for this session.

KNOW THE STORY

To understand the doctrine of humanity, we need to go back to the beginning. The Book of Genesis describes God's creation of the universe and our world—including human beings. It also shows us the exact moment when everything went wrong.

[25] So God made the wildlife of the earth according to their kinds, the livestock according to their kinds, and creatures that crawl on the ground according to their kinds. And God saw that it was good. [26] Then God said, "Let Us make man in Our image, according to Our likeness. They will rule the fish of the sea, the birds of the sky, the livestock, all the earth, and the creatures that crawl on the earth." [27] So God created man in His own image; He created him in the image of God; He created them male and female.
GENESIS 1:25-27

[1] Now the serpent was the most cunning of all the wild animals that the LORD God had made. He said to the woman, "Did God really say, 'You can't eat from any tree in the garden'?" [2] The woman said to the serpent, "We may eat the fruit from the trees in the garden. [3] But about the fruit of the tree in the middle of the garden, God said, 'You must not eat it or touch it, or you will die.'" [4] "No! You will not die," the serpent said to the woman. [5] "In fact, God knows that when you eat it your eyes will be opened and you will be like God, knowing good and evil." [6] Then the woman saw that the tree was good for food and delightful to look at, and that it was desirable for obtaining wisdom. So she took some of its fruit and ate it; she also gave some to her husband, who was with her, and he ate it.
GENESIS 3:1-6

What do you like best about our world? Why?

In what ways has sin most dramatically affected your family?

UNPACK THE STORY

EXPLORING HUMAN DIGNITY

When we think about the creation of human beings, and even what it means to be human, Genesis 1:25-26 offers a key distinction:

> [25] So God made the wildlife of the earth according to their kinds, the livestock according to their kinds, and creatures that crawl on the ground according to their kinds. And God saw that it was good. [26] Then God said, "Let Us make man in Our image, according to Our likeness. They will rule the fish of the sea, the birds of the sky, the livestock, all the earth, and the creatures that crawl on the earth."
> **GENESIS 1:25-26**

When God created the animals, He created them "according to their kinds." And as He created, He developed new and distinct patterns so that each type of animal was designed according to its own kind.

Things were different when God created human beings. In that case, He didn't create a new mold or pattern. Instead, He made humans according to *His own* kind. God created us as a reflection of Himself—of His own image. In other words, God was the pattern. This is what makes people distinctly different from the rest of creation but at the same time clearly a part of it. We are higher than the animals, yet still not God. This truth guides our understanding through the rest of God's Word because it helps us know who we are and what our purpose is.

Even better, these verses teach us about our value. Because we are created in God's image, we have dignity. We have worth. Unrelated to anything we do or will do—without any asterisks or caveats—we have value because we are reflections of God.

Because we are created in God's image, we have dignity. We have worth. Unrelated to anything we do or will do—without any asterisks or caveats—we have value because we are reflections of God.

What are the implications of people being made in the image of God?

How should this truth influence our actions and attitudes?

EXPLORING HUMAN DEPRAVITY

While mankind was created in dignity, it didn't last. Human dignity was quickly marred by depravity, which is the presence of sin. Just as Jeremiah's clay was marred in the potter's hands, our lives have been corrupted by disobedience and sin.

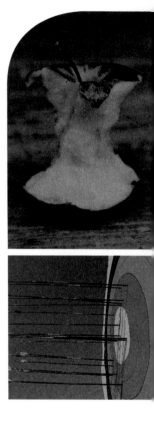

What comes to mind when you hear the word "sin"? Why?

The ancient Hebrew word translated as *sin* is actually an archery term. It means "to miss the mark" or "to fall short of the goal." When we disobey God, we miss the mark of His intended purpose for our lives. We fall short of God's plan.

And there are consequences.

Read Romans 3:23; Ephesians 2:1-3; and Colossians 2:13a. Then describe the consequences of sin in our lives.

Sin is like a virus that has infected every person. It's a global epidemic. While God created human beings as "good" and with the wonderful capacity to know Him, enjoy Him, serve Him and love Him, sin distorted who we are. People are now depraved. We are corrupt morally and wayward from God.

The result of our sin is separation from God in this life and divine judgment for our sin in the next. There is nothing we can do to change ourselves or save ourselves. Only Someone from outside of this sinful world can save us.

> There is nothing we can do to change ourselves or save ourselves. Only Someone from outside of this sinful world can save us.

Continue reading Romans 3:23-24; Ephesians 2:4-5; and Colossians 2:13b. Then discuss the solution each passage offers for the problem of sin.

ENGAGE

As you continue to study the major doctrines of the Christian faith, you'll benefit from finding ways to identify and apply those doctrines in everyday life. With that in mind, work with your group to assess the Bible's claims about humanity in light of current events.

Use the following questions to gauge how well the doctrine of humanity compares with what is happening in the world today. Consider looking through news sources (in print or online) in order to identify current events that reflect the human condition, both positive and negative. Examples could include anything from trials, crimes, and diseases all the way to prizes, works of art, and displays of heroism. (Note: if you don't have any news sources available, consider engaging this activity on your own in the next few days.)

Where do you see the dignity of humanity reflected in current events?

Where do you see the depravity of humanity reflected in current events?

PRAYER REQUESTS

....

....

....

....

....

....

....

....

....

....

In addition to studying God's Word, work with your group leader to create a plan for personal study, worship, and application between now and the next session. Select from the following optional activities to match your personal preferences and available time.

⬆ Worship

☑ Read your Bible. Complete the reading plan on page 30.

☐ Spend time with God by engaging the devotional experience on page 31.

☐ Take a walk this week and enjoy God's creation. Then sit down and craft your own psalm of worship to God.

➡ ⬅ Personal Study

☐ Read and interact with "Everyone Is Valuable" on page 32.

☐ Read and interact with "Everything Is Worship" on page 34.

⬅ ➡ Application

☐ Take time this week to share with someone your personal faith story. Start by telling them what your life was like before you met Jesus. Then tell them how you came to faith in Christ. Follow that with the difference Jesus has made in your life today.

☐ Take a moment to journal about the following: King David was confronted by his own personal sin. In a dramatic moment, the cover up of his elicit affair and the murder of Bathsheba's husband was exposed. There was nowhere to hide. In that moment, David was a broken man. He poured out his heart to God in his own personal journal. Read Psalm 51. How did David see his sin? What did he say to God? Take a moment to write your own journal entry of confession to God.

☐ Memorize Romans 3:23: "For all have sinned and fall short of the glory of God."

☐ Other:

 **WORSHIP**

READING PLAN

Read through the following Scripture passages this week. Use the space provided to record your thoughts and responses.

Day 1
Genesis 1:24-31

Day 2
Psalm 8:1-9

Day 3
Romans 7:13-25

Day 4
Isaiah 43:1-7

Day 5
Psalm 139:1-24

Day 6
Ephesians 4:17-24

Day 7
Psalm 119:73-80

PRONE TO WANDER

"We all went astray like sheep; we all have turned to our own way."
ISAIAH 53:6

Sheep have a tendency to wander. No matter how you speak to them, no matter how you train them, they are innately prone to wander away from their shepherd. In many ways, people act the same way. We also are prone to wander.

Robert Robinson grew up in a broken family. His father died when he was young, and he was sent out to work hard labor jobs early in life. He fell into the wrong crowd and soon ran the streets with wild company. It is said, that night as he and his friends were harassing an old gypsy woman, she pointed at Robert and said, "You will live to see your children and grandchildren." That got his attention. He thought, *If I'm going to live to see my children and grandchildren, I need to change the way I'm living.*

On another occasion, Robinson joined his friends to hear George Whitefield speak. They went with the intention of heckling the crowd, but that night Robert heard the gospel of Jesus Christ for the first time. He surrendered his life to the Savior. Two years later, in 1757, Robinson wrote down the lyrics to a hymn that is still sung in churches today: "Come, Thou Fount of Every Blessing."

In the last stanza, Robert wrote these words:

> Prone to wander, Lord, I feel it,
> Prone to leave the God I love;
> Here's my heart, Lord, take and seal it,
> Seal it for Thy courts above.[1]

Like Robert, and like sheep, there is something inside all human beings that causes us to drift from God. Our sin veers us off course and lures us from the One we love.

Describe a time in your life when you have wandered from God.

How has God brought you back to Himself?

EVERYONE IS VALUABLE

Many people think the sole purpose of Genesis 1–2 is to tell us how old the earth is. Simply put, Genesis isn't given to us for that. It isn't given to us to understand *how* or *when* the world was created. It's given to us to tell us *Who* created the universe and *why* He created it. Take a closer look at Genesis 1:26-28.

> 26 Then God said, "Let Us make man in Our image, according to Our likeness. They will rule the fish of the sea, the birds of the sky, the livestock, all the earth, and the creatures that crawl on the earth." 27 So God created man in His own image; He created him in the image of God; He created them male and female. 28 God blessed them, and God said to them, "Be fruitful, multiply, fill the earth, and subdue it. Rule the fish of the sea, the birds of the sky, and every creature that crawls on the earth."
> **GENESIS 1:26-28**

What would you identify as the primary theme of these verses?

Notice that this was the first time in the creation account that God said "Let Us." The Father, Son, and Holy Spirit are involved in the creation of mankind. There isn't just a physical creation happening here. There's spiritual creation happening as well. You are physical like the animals, but don't forget you are also spiritual—patterned after God to do something higher than the animals. But what does it mean to be patterned after God or created in the "image of God"? Consider the following statements.

People are created in God's image mentally. Just as God is rational, volitional, and communicative, mankind was created to reason, choose, and communicate. Every time a person thinks through a problem, chooses a course of action, or crafts a painting, he or she is reflecting the image of God.

People are created in God's image morally. Just as God is holy (see Isa. 6:3), righteous (see Ps. 145:17), just (see 2 Thess. 1:6), and good (see Ps. 136:1), God created mankind with a "moral compass" to choose right from wrong—a conscience (see Rom. 2:15) to make moral choices.

People are created in God's image socially. Just as God exists in community as the Trinity (Father, Son, and Spirit), God created people to live in community. The declaration that it was "not good for the man to be alone" (Gen. 2:18) represents our need for relationships with other people and with God. We can know God in a personal way and can choose to talk to Him in prayer, worship Him, serve Him, and obey Him.

People are created in God's image eternally. Just as God is eternal, mankind was created to live eternally. Although people have a finite beginning, each person is created with a living soul (Gen. 2:7), an immaterial part of his or her being that will live forever either with God or apart from God.

> *Which of the previous statements do you find the most difficult to believe? Why?*

The dignity of mankind is that God has personally, uniquely, and purposefully created each person for His own pleasure and for His own glory (see Isa. 43:7). Every person matters to God (see Matt. 10:31). Every person possesses the image of God (see Gen. 1:26). Every person is a divinely-crafted masterpiece (see Eph. 2:10). Every person is loved by God (see John 3:16). Every person finds satisfaction and joy in knowing God and fulfilling the purpose for which God has given his or her life.

So there is good news and bad news. You've already heard the good news: every single person is valuable—without a caveat and regardless of what we believe about God or what we've done—because we all are created in God's image.

That's good news. The bad news is that every person you hate, disagree with, can't stand to be around, that's ever hurt you, lied to you, manipulated you, or disagreed with you—they are valuable as well. We don't get to believe that some people are image bearers of God and are valuable, while others are not.

And anytime we disagree with that in our actions or words, we are marring the image of God.

> *Do you have trouble believing the previous statement? Why or why not?*

If every person was created by God and matters to God, then every person deserves to be treated with dignity and respect.

> *What are some ways you can demonstrate dignity and respect to those who have fallen through the cracks in your community?*

EVERYTHING IS WORSHIP

We have already established that because humans are all image bearers of God, everyone has value and is significant. If this is true and we are all significant, then everything we do is significant. Everything we do carries meaning. Everything is worship.

This is another good news/bad news situation. The good news is that nothing you do is unimportant. And isn't that attractive? Don't we all want who we are and what we do to count? If this is true, everything you do is designed to picture something true about God.

> The LORD God took the man and placed him in the garden of Eden
> to work it and watch over it.
> **GENESIS 2:15**

God put the man in this perfect garden and his purpose was to work and keep it. This is a loaded verse. The words *placed, work,* and *watch* have much deeper meanings than simply "God set them down in the garden and then had them tilling the soil and growing plants." The word *placed* means to set at rest. It's a peaceful term. It's like when you (against all your better judgment about how you'll be late, or how messy you'll get, or how risky it is) turn around on the interstate to go back and help that person change their flat tire in the pouring rain. You drive away soaked and late to your appointment with no perceivable benefit to you at all, and you still think, *That was what I was supposed to do.* When God placed the man in the garden, He was setting him at rest—at peace. And what He gave him to do didn't disrupt that rest—it's the very expression of it. See, God told the man to "work it and watch over it"—essentially to worship and obey. This is the expression of deepest rest. The way you are most human, both physical and spiritual, is to worship and obey in whatever state or environment you might find yourself in. This is what it means to reflect God's image. This is what it means to experience His "this is who I'm supposed to be" kind of rest. This is done by worshiping and obeying our Creator.

> **What observations stand out to you the most about this explanation of Genesis 2:15?**

That's the good news. Everything is important because everything is worship. The bad news is this: we're all blowing it. The word *worship* comes from the old English word *worth-ship.* In other words, what you worship is whatever has ultimate worth in your life. Worshiping God simply means that you put ultimate weight on what He says about you, about life, and about the world. You then put your trust in Him and obey Him.

And though we all worship, most of us end up worshiping ourselves. Worshiping yourself just means the ultimate weight goes onto you—about who you say you are and who you say other people are. But if all of our lives are supposed to reflect God's image, and our ultimate rest comes from believing that God is the only one worthy of obeying, then not a single thing we do should be separated from showing that worth. First Corinthians 10:31 says, "Therefore, whether you eat or drink, or whatever you do, do everything for God's glory." Remember, everything you do is spiritual. It's heavy. It's important.

What questions come to mind when reading that everything you do has weight and significance?

Paul Tripp describes our worship in this way:

"Human beings were created by God to be worshipers. You can't divide people into two groups, as if there are some who worship and others who don't. Every person, regardless of religious profession, has worshiped their way through every day of their existence. I would even argue that everything you say and everything you do is an act of worship. ... Romans 1:25 is probably the best diagnosis on our worship condition. It says that human beings will exchange the worship of the Creator for worship of created things. ... How are you doing in awareness? Are you sensitive to each opportunity you have to worship in word and deed? And how are you doing in action? Are you frequently exchanging the worship of God for worship of created things? For the child of God, life in a fallen world will be one big worship war. Even though we've been given the Holy Spirit and the ability to worship the Creator at all times, our sinful nature will fight to worship the created world."[2]

From Paul Tripp's quote, what application can you make to your life today?

1. Robert Robinsen, "Come, Thou Fount of Every Blessing," Baptist Hymnal (Nashville, TN: LifeWay Worship, 2008), 98.
2. Paul Tripp, "Worship Everyday," *paultripp.com*. Posted July 14, 2014. Accessed April 24, 2105.

THE PERSON AND WORK OF CHRIST

Jesus is God who reconciles us back to God

REFLECT

We saw in the previous session that human beings were created in God's image and designed to live in relationship with Him. Sadly, God's original plan was corrupted by the presence of sin. Our connection with God has been severed, and there's nothing we can do to fix it on our own. Thankfully, that reality points us to Jesus.

As you prepare to explore both the Person and work of Christ, take a moment to reflect on your experiences in recent days.

Which of the assignments did you explore this week? How did it go?

What did you learn or experience while reading the Bible?

What questions would you like to ask?

PRAY

Take a break from your discussion and approach God together in prayer. Use the following guidelines as you connect with Him:

- As a group, acknowledge the presence of sin in your lives. Take a moment to silently confess your sin before engaging the Scriptures.

- Ask for a greater awareness of the Spirit's presence as you explore God's Word together.

- Praise Jesus for the good news of the gospel and the ways He has changed your life.

INTRODUCTION

Many different people have been influential on a grand scale throughout human history. As we look back across the centuries, we are indebted to men and women who literally changed the course not only of civilizations, but of the entire world.

For example, think back to Alexander the Great. Tutored by Aristotle, a famous philosopher, Alexander has a convincing claim as the most successful military tactician in the history of the world. By the time he died in his early 30's, Alexander was undefeated in battle and had conquered a huge territory stretching from Egypt and Greece all the way to the borders of India. Even after his death, Alexander's work was vital in spreading Greek culture throughout much of the world, and his conquests laid the foundation for the later rise of the Roman Empire.

Johannes Gutenberg was another hugely influential figure in history, although his contributions were much different than those of Alexander the Great. Gutenberg invented the movable type printing press in the middle of the 15th century, which ushered in a new era of mass communication, increased literacy, and the spread of radical ideas, such as Protestant theology and nation-based languages.

Moving closer to our time, Mare Curie serves as one of the world's most influential scientists. Marie was awarded the Nobel Prize on two separate occasions and in two separate fields—chemistry and physics. Her discoveries in radioactivity paved the way for modern practices such as x-ray machines and radiation therapy.

Who are some of your favorite people from history? Why?

Of course, thinking about important people in the past reminds us of an important truth: Jesus Christ is without a doubt the most influential person in the history of the world. As we'll see in the following pages, Jesus' impact in the world can be traced to both who He is and what He has done.

Where do you see evidence of Jesus' influence throughout the world today?

KNOW THE STORY

Everyone seems to have an opinion of who Jesus is and what He sought to accomplish during His time on earth. Fortunately, we don't have to rely on the opinions of others. Jesus Himself has revealed the truth throughout the Bible—including this declaration at the beginning of His public ministry:

16 He came to Nazareth, where He had been brought up. As usual, He entered the synagogue on the Sabbath day and stood up to read. 17 The scroll of the prophet Isaiah was given to Him, and unrolling the scroll, He found the place where it was written:

> 18 The Spirit of the Lord is on Me,
> because He has anointed Me
> to preach good news to the poor.
> He has sent Me
> to proclaim freedom to the captives
> and recovery of sight to the blind,
> to set free the oppressed,
> 19 to proclaim the year of the Lord's favor.

20 He then rolled up the scroll, gave it back to the attendant, and sat down. And the eyes of everyone in the synagogue were fixed on Him. 21 He began by saying to them, "Today as you listen, this Scripture has been fulfilled."
LUKE 4:16-21

28 When they heard this, everyone in the synagogue was enraged. 29 They got up, drove Him out of town, and brought Him to the edge of the hill that their town was built on, intending to hurl Him over the cliff. 30 But He passed right through the crowd and went on His way.
LUKE 4:28-30

What do these verses communicate about who Jesus is and what He does?

UNPACK THE STORY

JESUS IS FULLY GOD AND FULLY HUMAN

As we explore the Person of Jesus and attempt to identify who He is, one of the first truths we need to understand is that Jesus is both fully God and fully human. This can be a difficult concept to process. Fortunately, the Scriptures provide some concrete examples that highlight both elements of Jesus' nature.

In Luke 4, for example, we see evidence of Jesus' humanity. Verse 16 says Jesus came to the village of Nazareth, "where He had been brought up." Jesus had a hometown. He had neighbors. He was part of a community. What's more, Jesus had regular patterns and predictable routines:

> *As usual*, He entered the synagogue on the Sabbath day and stood up to read.
> **LUKE 4:16b, emphasis added**

> Jesus had a hometown. He had neighbors. He was part of a community. What's more, Jesus had regular patterns and predictable routines.

Why is it important to understand that Jesus was fully human?

Luke 4 also provides two interesting pictures of Jesus' divinity—the first of which was initiated by Jesus Himself. After being handed a scroll containing the Book of Isaiah, Jesus chose to read a prophecy about the Messiah. Each of His hearers would have been familiar with this passage, and each would have longed for the prophecy to be fulfilled. So, even reading the passage was suggestive on Jesus' behalf. Yet Jesus left no doubt about His intentions when He declared: "Today as you listen, this Scripture has been fulfilled" (v. 21).

The second illustration of Jesus' divinity came when He miraculously passed through an angry mob. The text makes it clear that the people of Jesus' hometown were enraged to the point of murder (see v. 29). Yet Jesus passed through them as if they weren't even there. Interestingly, the people weren't angry that Jesus declared Himself the Messiah. Instead, they were enraged at the notion of God accepting the Gentiles and rejecting His chosen people (see vv. 24-30).

Why is it important to understand that Jesus was fully God?

JESUS ACCOMPLISHES OUR SALVATION

Now that we have a greater understanding of Jesus' identity—of who He is—let's take a moment to consider what He does on our behalf. Once again, we have the benefit of Jesus' own words to get us started:

> 18 The Spirit of the Lord is on Me,
> because He has anointed Me
> to preach good news to the poor.
> He has sent Me
> to proclaim freedom to the captives
> and recovery of sight to the blind,
> to set free the oppressed,
> 19 to proclaim the year of the Lord's favor.
> **LUKE 4:18-19**

How have you seen these verses fulfilled through Jesus' life and ministry?

On the surface, Jesus' words seem to focus primarily on social issues—good news for the poor, freedom for the captives, sight for the blind, and relief for the oppressed. And it's certainly true that Jesus' ministry in the world has accomplished these goals throughout Christian history.

However, it's vital to understand that Jesus had a deeper meaning in mind. The people of Jesus' day believed the Messiah would restore the glory of Israel in a blaze of military and political power. Yet Jesus knew that His mission was primarily spiritual. He came to proclaim the good news of redemption, to free all people from their captivity to sin, to heal our spiritual blindness, and to set us free from the oppression of our own flesh.

In other words, Jesus came to accomplish our salvation.

How have you personally benefited from Jesus' ministry?

Jesus came to proclaim the good news of redemption, to free all people from their captivity to sin, to heal our spiritual blindness, and to set us free from the oppression of our own flesh.

ENGAGE

One of the important elements involved with studying Christian doctrine is learning to identify teachings and statements that are incorrect. This is especially important in connection with the doctrine of Christ. Throughout history, there have been many false teachers who have spread heresy regarding the Person and work of Jesus. Many of these false doctrines still exist today.

With that in mind, work as a group to answer the following questions.

What are some false teachings about Jesus that remain popular in today's culture? Make a list, if possible.

What steps can we take to properly evaluate different teachings in order to determine whether they are true or false?

PRAYER REQUESTS

....

....

....

....

....

....

....

....

....

....

....

....

In addition to studying God's Word, work with your group leader to create a plan for personal study, worship, and application between now and the next session. Select from the following optional activities to match your personal preferences and available time.

⬆ Worship

☑ Read your Bible. Complete the reading plan on page 44.

☐ Spend time with God by engaging the devotional experience on page 45.

☐ Connect with God each day through prayer.

➡ ⬅ Personal Study

☐ Read and interact with "Fully Human and Fully God" on page 46.

☐ Read and interact with "Our Salvation" on page 48.

⬅ ➡ Application

☐ Pray at the beginning of each day that God would open the door for you to share the truth about Jesus with someone who needs to hear it. Keep your eyes open throughout the day for possible answers to your prayers.

☐ Memorize Hebrews 4:15: "For we do not have a high priest who is unable to sympathize with our weaknesses, but One who has been tested in every way as we are, yet without sin."

☐ When you have an opportunity to participate in Jesus' mission this week, invite another disciple to join you.

☐ Deepen your knowledge of Christian doctrine by seeking more information on the Person and work of Jesus. Read a book, download a podcast, listen to a sermon, etc.

☐ Other:

 **WORSHIP**

READING PLAN

Read through the following Scripture passages this week. Use the space provided to record your thoughts and responses.

Day 1
Isaiah 11:1-9

Day 2
Luke 1:26-56

Day 3
John 1:1-18

Day 4
John 19:1-42

Day 5
Philippians 2:1-11

Day 6
Hebrews 2:1-18

Day 7
Revelation 1:1-20

POSITION AND PRACTICE

We often think of Christian doctrines as abstract concepts—complicated theories that don't really apply to everyday life. This isn't true, of course. The doctrines of the Christian faith are essential to everyday life because they help us understand who we are, who we were meant to be, and how we are called to live in service to God. In many ways, Christian doctrine is the foundation of everyday life for a disciple of Christ.

The good news is that doctrine doesn't have to be complicated. Because the doctrines have practical application in our lives, they can be understood in practical terms. For example, consider the following chart as a way of explaining the salvation Christ has accomplished for us:

	Position *What God Sees*	Practice *What We Are*
Non-Christian	Sinful	Sinful
Christian	Righteous	Sinful
Glorified Christian	Righteous	Righteous

As you can see from the chart, all people are defined by their sinful condition before they receive the gift of salvation offered by Jesus. Before we know Christ, we are sinful in what we do and sinful in God's eyes.

When we encounter Jesus, however, something vital changes in our position with God. We continue to practice sin as we go about our lives—Christians don't become perfect when they follow Christ. But because Jesus has taken the penalty for our sins, we are forgiven in our position before God. In fact, when God looks at us, He doesn't see our failing bodies and corrupted minds. Instead, He sees the righteousness of Christ. That's the miracle known as the doctrine of salvation.

Finally, when we shed our sinful flesh through death, we take up new life with Christ in heaven—a process known as "glorification." In this new life, we not only have the position of righteousness in God's eyes, but we also practice righteousness in every moment of our lives. We become like Jesus.

How should the doctrine of salvation influence your actions and attitudes each day?

FULLY HUMAN AND FULLY GOD

We use a number of different titles in today's culture for different things. Most of these titles are connected with our jobs—with the things we do. Think of "doctor," "professor," and "judge," for example. People used titles in the ancient world, as well. However, those titles were often connected to who a person was, rather than what a person did. A person's title was a key element of his or her identity.

With that in mind, we can further explore the nature of Jesus' character and identity by focusing on two titles commonly used to identify Him throughout the Scriptures: "Son of God" and "Son of Man."

First, let's look at "Son of God." Interestingly, Jesus rarely used this title when referencing Himself. Instead, others often applied this title to Jesus in order to identify His divine heritage.

> *Read the following passages of Scripture and identify those who proclaimed Jesus to be the "Son of God":*
>
> *Luke 1:35*
>
> *Luke 4:40-41*
>
> *Luke 22:66-71*
>
> *John 1:43-51*

In the culture of Jesus' day, society was heavily influenced by the concepts of sonship and inheritance. Specifically, the eldest son in a family was the primary heir of his father, which meant he carried his father's status and authority. To call Jesus the "Son of God," then, was to give Jesus the same level of honor and authority as God.

Essentially, the title "Son of God" was a declaration that Jesus was equal with God. Given the context of the rest of the Bible, we can say with certainty that Jesus *is* God.

> *Take a moment to skim through the Gospel of Matthew. What evidence do you see to support the claim that Jesus is God?*

Now let's take a deeper look at Jesus' second title: "Son of Man." This was actually the title Jesus used most often when referring to Himself. For example:

> ²⁶ It must not be like that among you. On the contrary, whoever wants to become great among you must be your servant, ²⁷ and whoever wants to be first among you must be your slave; ²⁸ just as the Son of Man did not come to be served, but to serve, and to give His life— a ransom for many.
> **MATTHEW 20:26-28**

"Son of Man" emphasizes Jesus' humanity. The title reminds us that since Jesus has a physical body like ours, He also shares our weakness, our frailty, and even our suffering. No pain we experience is unfamiliar to our Lord, and no problem we encounter is too big for His power.

> ¹⁴ Therefore, since we have a great high priest who has passed through the heavens—Jesus the Son of God—let us hold fast to the confession. ¹⁵ For we do not have a high priest who is unable to sympathize with our weaknesses, but One who has been tested in every way as we are, yet without sin.
> **HEBREWS 4:14-15**

How does Jesus' humanity impact your life today?

CASE STUDY: Imagine that a Christian friend of yours has recently been diagnosed with cancer. This friend is facing the real possibility of death and therefore is in great despair.

How would you comfort your friend with the truth that Jesus is fully human?

How would you comfort your friend with the truth that Jesus is fully God?

PERSONAL STUDY

OUR SALVATION

We've seen that Jesus is both fully human and fully God. He is the "Son of God" and the "Son of Man." This can be a difficult concept to understand in full, but it's a concept that has a vital impact on our spiritual lives. Consider the following:

> 32 As for Me, if I am lifted up from the earth I will draw all people to Myself." 33 He said this to signify what kind of death He was about to die. 34 Then the crowd replied to Him, "We have heard from the scripture that the Messiah will remain forever. So how can You say, 'The Son of Man must be lifted up'? Who is this Son of Man?" 35 Jesus answered, "The light will be with you only a little longer. Walk while you have the light so that darkness doesn't overtake you. The one who walks in darkness doesn't know where he's going. 36 While you have the light, believe in the light so that you may become sons of light."
> **JOHN 12:32-36a, emphasis added**

> 16 "For God loved the world in this way: He gave His One and Only Son, so that everyone who believes in Him will not perish but have eternal life. 17 For God did not send His Son into the world that He might condemn the world, but that the world might be saved through Him. 18 Anyone who believes in Him is not condemned, but anyone who does not believe is already condemned, because he has not believed in the name of *the One and Only Son of God.*
> **JOHN 3:16-18, emphasis added**

Jesus' dual nature is a necessary foundation for our salvation. Without His full humanity and full divinity, we would be lost.

Why is Jesus' humanity a necessary element of our salvation?

Why is Jesus' divinity a necessary element of our salvation?

These point back to an Old-Testament event called the Day of Atonement. On this day each year, the high priest chose a lamb upon which to place all the sins of all the people of Israel. This lamb was then sent out to die in the wilderness, bearing away the sins of the people and leaving them clean before God.

This was a ritual, of course. There wasn't anything special about the lamb chosen each year, nor did the priest have any real power to offer forgiveness. Instead, the ritual pointed forward to the coming Someone who *was* special and who *did* have power: Jesus Christ.

With that in mind, look at what John the Baptist said when he first encountered Jesus:

> ²⁹ The next day John saw Jesus coming toward him and said, "Here is the Lamb of God, who takes away the sin of the world! ³⁰ This is the One I told you about: 'After me comes a man who has surpassed me, because He existed before me.'"
> **JOHN 1:29-30**

How do these verses contribute to your understanding of salvation?

The doctrine of atonement is easy to remember when you break it into parts: "at-one-ment." In that single moment ("ment") when Jesus died on the cross, He made us "at one" with God by bearing the punishment for our sins.

Again, it's important to see that only Jesus could accomplish such a feat. Because Jesus is fully human, He was able to take our sins upon Himself—and to die because of it. Yet, since Jesus is fully God, He is larger even than our sins. His power as God allowed Him to absorb our punishment and still rise victorious from the grave.

What steps can you take to worship and thank Jesus for His accomplishments as part of your daily life?

THE KINGDOM OF GOD

God's kingdom includes the "now and not yet" reign of King Jesus.

REFLECT

We saw in the previous session that Jesus Christ is both fully human and fully God. This dual nature is at the core of Christ's identity, and it points to His primary reason for coming to earth: securing our salvation. Jesus alone accomplishes salvation for those within God's kingdom.

But what *is* God's kingdom? That's the focus of this session. Before we dive in, however, take a moment to discuss your recent experiences.

Which of the assignments did you explore this week? How did it go?

What did you learn or experience while reading the Bible?

What questions would you like to ask?

PRAY

Take a break from your discussion and approach God together in prayer. Use the following guidelines as you connect with Him:

- As a group, take a moment to praise and honor Jesus as the King of the universe.

- Confess that you often live as if you were outside of God's kingdom—as if you were king of your life, rather than God. Ask Him to forgive your sins.

- Ask for wisdom as you study what it means to live as a member of God's kingdom and help advance His kingdom in the world.

INTRODUCTION

How many kingdoms are you in charge of? Unless you're currently leading one of the 40 or so monarchies in existence throughout the world, your first answer to that question is probably, "None." But don't be so sure!

In its truest form, a "kingdom" is simply any place in which a person's will is done. If a man is in charge of a country—if his will is carried out within its borders—that country is his kingdom. In the same way, if a businesswoman is in charge of a company, that company is essentially her kingdom. An estate owner who tells resources where to go and what to do has a kingdom. Even a child who is allowed to make decisions about his or her bedroom has a tiny kingdom.

In short, wherever your will is carried out, that is your kingdom.

What are some "kingdoms" you're in charge of?

What have you learned or been taught about the kingdom of God?

As we think about the kingdom of God, the same definition for *kingdom* applies. Therefore, God's kingdom exists wherever His will is carried out. To say it in another way, the kingdom of God is simply the reign and rule of God over any area in which He has control.

That's why Jesus included these famous words in His model prayer:

> Your kingdom come.
> Your will be done
> on earth as it is in heaven.
> **MATTHEW 6:10**

As we explore the doctrine of God's kingdom throughout this session, we'll gain a greater understanding of what it means for God's kingdom to come both in this world and in the lives of those who follow Him.

KNOW THE STORY

Many people today feel confused about the kingdom of God. Does God's kingdom exist now, or is it something we will experience in the future? The people of Jesus' day had the same questions:

20 Being asked by the Pharisees when the kingdom of God will come, He answered them, "The kingdom of God is not coming with something observable; 21 no one will say, 'Look here!' or 'There!' For you see, the kingdom of God is among you."

22 Then He told the disciples: "The days are coming when you will long to see one of the days of the Son of Man, but you won't see it. 23 They will say to you, 'Look there!' or 'Look here!' Don't follow or run after them. 24 For as the lightning flashes from horizon to horizon and lights up the sky, so the Son of Man will be in His day. 25 But first He must suffer many things and be rejected by this generation.

26 "Just as it was in the days of Noah, so it will be in the days of the Son of Man: 27 People went on eating, drinking, marrying and giving in marriage until the day Noah boarded the ark, and the flood came and destroyed them all. 28 It will be the same as it was in the days of Lot: People went on eating, drinking, buying, selling, planting, building. 29 But on the day Lot left Sodom, fire and sulfur rained from heaven and destroyed them all. 30 It will be like that on the day the Son of Man is revealed. …

33 Whoever tries to make his life secure will lose it, and whoever loses his life will preserve it. 34 I tell you, on that night two will be in one bed: One will be taken and the other will be left. 35 Two women will be grinding grain together: One will be taken and the other left.
LUKE 17:20-30,33-35

What do these verses reveal about the kingdom of God?

UNPACK THE STORY

GOD'S KINGDOM IS "NOW AND NOT YET"

Jesus' interaction with the Pharisees in Luke 17 seems uncomplicated. For once, they asked Him a straightforward question: when will the kingdom of God come? And it seems as if Jesus gave them a straightforward answer: "the kingdom of God is among you" (v. 21). Yet, when Jesus turned to His disciples in verse 22, He proceeded to describe in some detail what it would be like when the kingdom of God comes in full.

So, what gives? The answer is that God's kingdom is both "now" and "not yet."

One of the core messages of the Bible is that sin has corrupted the relationship between God and humanity. Sin always goes against God's will, which means our sinfulness is a rejection of God's will. And because we have rejected God's will, we are in active rebellion against His kingdom. Remember, God's kingdom exists wherever His will is carried out.

However, sin has not removed everyone from God's kingdom. Beginning with the Israelites and extending to the church, God is carrying out His plan to restore His relationship with humanity by offering us atonement and salvation. When we repent of our sin and submit to Christ as our Lord and Savior, we're no longer in active rebellion against God. We are welcomed back into His kingdom with open arms.

When we repent of our sin and submit to Christ as our Lord and Savior, we're no longer in active rebellion against God. We are welcomed back into His kingdom with open arms.

What are the benefits and challenges of being members in God's kingdom?

The reason Jesus could say "the kingdom of God is among you" is because many people of His time had submitted to God's will. The same is true today, although on a larger scale—what we know as the church. Still, the majority of humanity remains in rebellion against God.

There will come a day, however, when all rebellion will end. God will once again establish His kingdom across the world. This is the time of judgment Jesus described to His disciples.

Look again at Luke 17:26-35. What emotions do you experience when you read these verses?

CHRISTIANS LIVE AS CITIZENS OF GOD'S KINGDOM

In teaching His disciples about the future revelation of God's kingdom, Jesus referenced two stories from the Old Testament that both paint a frightening picture.

Read Genesis 7:11-24; 19:12-26. What are your initial reactions to these passages?

By referencing the stories of Noah and Lot, Jesus was highlighting the sharp contrast between the kingdom of God and the kingdom of the world. In both stories, the majority of people were concerned only with worldly needs and desires: eating, drinking, marrying, buying, selling, planting, building, and so on. These aren't negative activities—they're not sinful in and of themselves—but they are entirely focused on temporary concerns.

Jesus' point is that people who focus only on earthly activities, ignoring God's will in the process, will be blindsided when the day of judgment arrives. In other words, those who belong to the kingdom of the world are ignorant of their spiritual danger because they care only about the kingdom of the world.

Luke 17:33 is the key: "Whoever tries to make his life secure will lose it, and whoever loses his life will preserve it." The only way to move from the kingdom of the world to the kingdom of God is to willingly surrender control of your life. To gain what is eternal, you must let go of everything that is temporary—everything this world cares so much about.

A Christian is any person who turns to Jesus and says, "Everything in my life is negotiable except You." That's what it means to live as a citizen of God's kingdom.

> A Christian is any person who turns to Jesus and says, "Everything in my life is negotiable except You."

What are the main values and concerns of modern culture?

When have you had trouble submitting control over a specific area of your life?

When have you been victorious at breaking free from the kingdom of the world?

ENGAGE

One of the main blessings of studying God's Word as part of a community is that you get the benefit of searching for truth together. As the saying goes, two heads are better than one—and several heads are even better than two. With that in mind, work as a group to compare and contrast the values of God's kingdom with the values of the world's kingdom.

Use the chart below to organize your discussion. What are the main goals or ambitions for each kingdom in connection with the following areas of life:

	Kingdom of God	Kingdom of the World
Marriage		
Parenting		
Friendship		
Work		
Career		
Finances		
Entertainment		

PRAYER REQUESTS

....

....

....

....

....

....

....

....

In addition to studying God's Word, work with your group leader to create a plan for personal study, worship, and application between now and the next session. Select from the following optional activities to match your personal preferences and available time.

↑ Worship

☑ Read your Bible. Complete the reading plan on page 58.

☐ Spend time with God by engaging the devotional experience on page 59.

☐ Connect with God each day through prayer.

➡ ⬅ Personal Study

☐ Read and interact with "God's Kingdom Is 'Now and Not Yet'" on page 60.

☐ Read and interact with "Christians Live as Citizens of God's Kingdom" on page 62.

⬅ ➡ Application

☐ Be intentional about making the most of your experiences at church this weekend. Take advantage of opportunities to engage other disciples of Jesus in a more meaningful way.

☐ Memorize John 1:29: "The next day John saw Jesus coming toward him and said, 'Here is the Lamb of God, who takes away the sin of the world!'"

☐ When you have an opportunity to participate in Jesus' mission this week, invite another disciple to join you.

☐ Start a journal to record the different ways you engage Jesus' mission for the world each day. This is a great way to remind yourself of that mission and evaluate your participation in it.

☐ Other:

 **WORSHIP**

READING PLAN

Read through the following Scripture passages this week. Use the space provided to record your thoughts and responses.

Day 1
Genesis 12:1-9

Day 2
Jeremiah 31:31-40

Day 3
Daniel 2:27-45

Day 4
Matthew 6:19-34

Day 5
John 18:28-40

Day 6
1 Corinthians 15:50-58

Day 7
Revelation 22:1-21

THE MODEL PRAYER

We've seen how Jesus referenced God's will and God's kingdom in the model prayer He used to instruct His disciples. We typically refer to this prayer as the Lord's Prayer, and it has served as a guide to countless Jesus' followers throughout the centuries.

The version of Jesus' prayer found below is more compact than the one recorded in Matthew 6:9-13, but the vital elements are still there. Read this prayer out loud as an act of worship and obedience. As you do, focus on how the words apply to you specifically as a member of God's kingdom rather than the kingdom of the world.

> [1] He was praying in a certain place, and when He finished, one of His disciples said to Him, "Lord, teach us to pray, just as John also taught his disciples."
>
> [2] He said to them, "Whenever you pray, say:
>
> Father,
> Your name be honored as holy.
> Your kingdom come.
> [3] Give us each day our daily bread.
> [4] And forgive us our sins,
> for we ourselves also forgive everyone
> in debt to us.
> And do not bring us into temptation."
> **LUKE 11:1-4**

What emotions and/or memories come to mind when you read through this prayer?

How does this prayer guide your actions and attitudes as a member of God's kingdom?

GOD'S KINGDOM IS "NOW AND NOT YET"

As we've seen, if someone were to ask you the same question the Pharisees asked Jesus in Luke 17—When will the kingdom of God come to earth?—it would be hard for you to give a wrong answer. Throughout the Gospels, Jesus both spoke of God's kingdom as something that "is among you" and something that is yet to come. Accordingly, modern theologians have helpfully described God's kingdom as both "now and not yet."

The kingdom of God is already here in the sense that every Christian is a part of that kingdom. Those who follow God have placed their lives under the reign of King Jesus, and every church is an outpost of His kingdom. Yet God's kingdom is also obviously not yet here—not in full, at least. Our world is marked by pain, brokenness, wickedness, and death. It bears all the marks of still awaiting the rightful king's ascent to the throne.

Some day, King Jesus will return to finally conquer all His enemies and set up an eternal and perfect kingdom. While His kingdom is among us, that day is yet to come.

> *How has the presence of God's kingdom on earth benefited those who are not part of that kingdom?*

> *In what ways have you felt the tension of living in the world as a member of God's kingdom?*

This theme of "now and not yet" continues in the New Testament as we move beyond the Gospels:

> [17] Instruct those who are rich in the present age not to be arrogant or to set their hope on the uncertainty of wealth, but on God, who richly provides us with all things to enjoy. [18] Instruct them to do what is good, to be rich in good works, to be generous, willing to share, [19] storing up for themselves a good reserve for the age to come, so that they may take hold of life that is real.
> **1 TIMOTHY 6:17-19**

Here again we have two specific periods of time: "the present age" and "the age to come." Paul warned his readers against living as if the present age was all that mattered. Instead, he encouraged them to set their priorities based on the age to come.

Paul offered similar instructions to Titus, another one of his disciples:

> 11 For the grace of God has appeared with salvation for all people, 12 instructing us to deny godlessness and worldly lusts and to live in a sensible, righteous, and godly way in the present age, 13 while we wait for the blessed hope and appearing of the glory of our great God and Savior, Jesus Christ. 14 He gave Himself for us to redeem us from all lawlessness and to cleanse for Himself a people for His own possession, eager to do good works.
> **TITUS 2:11-14**

What are some expectations from these Scripture passages that you can apply in your everyday life?

It's important to remember that our world is currently in a time of transition. When Jesus came to earth in human form (what we call the incarnation), He began the process of moving the world out of the present age and into the age to come. It's been a long process. Two thousand years later, society is still broken—still suffering the pains of the present age—and yet every day God's people join in His work to advance His kingdom further and deeper into the world.

When Jesus returns to the earth, He will complete the process. His return will end the present age and finally establish the age to come in fullness and glory. Until that day comes, however, the world will remain caught in the tension between the "now" and the "not yet." And so will we.

What disciplines and practices will help you live well in the tension between the present age and the age to come?

CHRISTIANS LIVE AS CITIZENS OF GOD'S KINGDOM

To be a Christian is to gladly place every area of your life under the reign of King Jesus—to kneel before Him and say, "Everything in my life is negotiable except You." That's the price of citizenship in the kingdom of God. But what do we gain? What are the benefits of membership in God's kingdom?

The apostle John gave us a glimpse of what it means to enjoy life in the kingdom of God.

¹ Then I saw a new heaven and a new earth, for the first heaven and the first earth had passed away, and the sea no longer existed. ² I also saw the Holy City, new Jerusalem, coming down out of heaven from God, prepared like a bride adorned for her husband.

³ Then I heard a loud voice from the throne:

Look! God's dwelling is with humanity,
and He will live with them.
They will be His people,
and God Himself will be with them
and be their God.
⁴ He will wipe away every tear from their eyes.
Death will no longer exist;
grief, crying, and pain will exist no longer,
because the previous things have passed away.
REVELATION 21:1-4

What emotions do you experience when you read these verses?

John was describing heaven, of course. God gave him a vision, a glimpse, of what life will be like when God's will is fully accomplished throughout the universe—when His kingdom comes to earth without rebellion, corruption, or compromise.

This is our future as followers of God and members of His kingdom. This is what we look forward to as we live and minister in this present age of sin.

Until that day comes, however, we have work to do. Being a member of God's kingdom is not a passive experience—at least, it shouldn't be. We are not simply passengers on a cruise-liner called Earth, waiting in comfort until we arrive at our heavenly destination.

Instead, God has called us to give our time, talents, energy, resources, and even our very lives—all for the goal of advancing His kingdom in the world.

> *Read the following passages of Scripture and record what they teach about our responsibilities as earthly members of God's kingdom.*
>
> *Matthew 22:37-40*
>
> *Matthew 28:18-20*
>
> *John 17:20-26*
>
> *Acts 1:4-8*

Of course, there are also immediate benefits to being citizens of God's kingdom. We are blessed with the forgiveness of our sins, for example. We can experience the joy of true community. And we have the unbelievable privilege of connecting with and relating to the Creator of the universe.

Case Study: Imagine you are speaking with a friend about what it means to be a Christian—a citizen of God's kingdom. How would you answer the following questions?

> *What are Christians supposed to do?*
>
> *What are Christians not supposed to do?*

THE DOCTRINE OF THE HOLY SPIRIT

The Spirit empowers God's people to live for Jesus

REFLECT

In the previous session we explored the definition of God's kingdom as a "now and not yet" reality. We saw that God's kingdom is present on earth whenever people are in submission to His will, yet will not become fully manifest in the universe until the day of judgment. Until that occurs, Christians have a responsibility to help advance God's kingdom as citizens.

Before we engage the doctrine of the Holy Spirit, take a few moments to reflect on and discuss your recent experiences.

Which of the assignments did you explore this week? How did it go?

What did you learn or experience while reading the Bible?

What questions would you like to ask?

PRAY

Begin the session by connecting with God through prayer. Use the following guidelines as you speak with Him:

- Thank God that He is at work in your life and in the world.

- Ask Him to speak to you today and open your eyes to how He works through the power of His Spirit.

- Pray that a biblical understanding of the Holy Spirit would be evident and encouraging over the next week of study.

INTRODUCTION

Did you know windmills have been around for centuries? They were first constructed in the region we call Iran today, and they date all the way back to 200 B.C. In recent years, windmills have become a major source of energy throughout the world. We usually refer to these modern creations as turbines, and they work to harness the invisible, weightless, formless, and powerful force of the wind.

Think about that for a moment. You can't see the wind, but you can see its effects. You can't grab the wind, but you can harness its great power. Jesus hinted at this reality during a conversation with a religious leader.

> The wind blows where it pleases, and you hear its sound, but you don't know where it comes from or where it is going. So it is with everyone born of the Spirit.
> **JOHN 3:8**

Like the wind, the Spirit of God is invisible, weightless, formless—and immeasurably powerful. Indeed, God created the world through the power of the Spirit. Jesus performed miracles, endured the cross, and rose from the dead in the power of the Spirit. And through that same power, God moves in the lives of people to know Him and to serve Him.

People are often confused about the Holy Spirit. Some have chosen to belittle the Spirit because they're skeptical or even uncomfortable about God moving in their lives. Others have abused the teaching of the Holy Spirit, making Him the focal point of their ministry and blaming the Spirit for all kinds of strange behavior. Still others have stayed away from the subject entirely because of theological disagreements.

What have you been taught about the role and work of the Holy Spirit?

In what ways have you experienced the Spirit in your life?

What we need today isn't less of God's Spirit, but more. We don't need to be afraid of the Spirit's power in our lives. Instead, we need more dependence on His power and His support as we seek to follow God.

KNOW THE STORY

Just before Jesus' death, He met with His disciples one last time. The shadow of the cross was looming and Jesus knew soon He would no longer be with them. Gathered around a table to share their last meal together, Jesus spoke words of comfort to His friends. He also spoke about the Spirit of God.

> [15] "If you love me, keep my commands. [16] And I will ask the Father, and he will give you another advocate to help you and be with you forever— [17] the Spirit of truth. The world cannot accept him, because it neither sees him nor knows him. But you know him, for he lives with you and will be in you. [18] I will not leave you as orphans; I will come to you. [19] Before long, the world will not see me anymore, but you will see me. Because I live, you also will live.
>
> **JOHN 14:15-19 (NIV)**

> [7] Nevertheless, I am telling you the truth. It is for your benefit that I go away, because if I don't go away the Counselor will not come to you. If I go, I will send Him to you. [8] When He comes, He will convict the world about sin, righteousness, and judgment: [9] About sin, because they do not believe in Me; [10] about righteousness, because I am going to the Father and you will no longer see Me; [11] and about judgment, because the ruler of this world has been judged.
>
> **JOHN 16:7-11**

What do these verses teach us about the Holy Spirit?

What questions would you like to ask about the role of the Spirit in this world?

God wants to be with you. He wants to walk with you throughout your day and never leave you. How is that possible? Because of the Holy Spirit! Through the Spirit, God has provided everything you need to know Him, follow Him, serve Him, love Him, and enjoy Him forever.

UNPACK THE STORY

WHO IS THE HOLY SPIRIT?

As with the other members of the Trinity, the best way to study the Holy Spirit is to answer two key questions. Here's the first: Who is the Holy Spirit? There are three main ways to answer that question, and all three are necessary for a proper understanding of God's Spirit.

1. The Holy Spirit is a Person. The Holy Spirit isn't a force. He's not energy in the universe or some kind of mystical power. The Holy Spirit is a Person. Jesus referred to the Spirit as "Him" or "He" six times in John 14:15-19. He is a Person. He speaks, prays, testifies, leads, commands, guides, and appoints. He can be grieved, lied to, insulted, or blasphemed. He has thoughts and desires. He makes decisions and has emotions.

How can we relate to the Spirit in a personal way?

The Holy Spirit isn't a force. He's not energy in the universe or some kind of mystical power. The Holy Spirit is a Person.

2. The Holy Spirit is God. The Holy Spirit is the third Person of the Trinity. Again, the Trinity is a hard concept to grasp—how can the Spirit be a separate Person from the Father and the Son, yet still part of one Being? We don't know for sure. We can't understand the Trinity in full. Still, we can trust what God has revealed in His Word.

3. The Holy Spirit is Truth. The Spirit is the Source of truth, and He guides you into all truth (see John 14:17). Specifically, the Spirit had a vital role in the creation of the Bible.

> [20] First of all, you should know this: No prophecy of Scripture comes from one's own interpretation, [21] because no prophecy ever came by the will of man; instead, men spoke from God as they were moved by the Holy Spirit.
> **2 PETER 1:20-21**

The reason you have a Bible is because of the Spirit's work revealing truth in a way you can understand it. But He not only reveals truth, He also leads you into truth. The Spirit points to Jesus who said, "I am the way, the truth, and the life" (John 14:6).

How does the Spirit help us engage the Scriptures today?

WHAT DOES THE SPIRIT DO?

Here's the second question: What does the Holy Spirit do? Let's look at two primary ways the Spirit works in our lives as we follow Christ.

1. The Holy Spirit facilitates salvation. Salvation is a work of the Spirit. Yes, salvation is centered on faith in Jesus Christ, but we need to understand that no one can be saved or come to know Jesus apart from the Spirit's work in his or her life. The Holy Spirit convicts us of our sin, points us to Christ, and reveals the truth of Jesus. It's through the Spirit that we pass from death to life in that wonderful moment we refer to as "being saved."

Look back at John 16:7-11. How have you seen these works of the Spirit on a large scale?

Looking at your own life, how did the Holy Spirit convict you of your sin and draw you to Jesus?

2. The Spirit produces transformation. Not only does the Holy Spirit facilitate your salvation, but He also transforms you to become more and more like Jesus. God loves you too much to leave you the way you are. His goal is to make you into a new person who reflects both the character and the priorities of Jesus.

Consider this quote from author Bill Bright:

> "The Spirit-filled Christian has given up his own powerless, defeated and fruitless life for the supernatural power, victory and fruitfulness of Jesus Christ. This is what we mean by the supernatural life. When a Christian is living supernaturally, he is filled with the Holy Spirit—filled with Jesus Christ, allowing God to work in Him and through him."[1]

God loves you too much to leave you the way you are. His goal is to make you into a new person who reflects both the character and the priorities of Jesus.

What steps can we take to more fully experience the Spirit's presence and power each day?

ENGAGE

Use the last part of your time together by splitting up into smaller groups and discussing more personal applications concerning the power of the Holy Spirit in your lives. Allow yourself to be open and honest about the following discussion points.

Discussion Point 1: We studied how the Spirit of God transforms our lives by promising to change us, lead us, and empower us. Share with your group an area where you need the Spirit to work in your life. For example, maybe you need Him to break a sinful habit, change an attitude, lead you in a decision, give you boldness, or empower you to serve God more fully. Talk these things through and pray for one another.

Discussion Point 2: Discuss what you've learned and how to put it into practice. The Spirit is always leading us to take action. In fact, the Book of Acts is really about the action of the Holy Spirit in the early church. Everywhere you turn in that book, the Spirit of God is moving! He is leading, directing, prompting, empowering, opening doors of opportunity and doing miraculous things. Discuss with your group what the Spirit of God is leading you to do. If you're not sure what that is yet, pray as a group for the Spirit to reveal to you what actions He wants you to take. Ask Him for boldness as you follow His lead.

PRAYER REQUESTS

....

....

....

....

....

....

....

....

....

....

1. Bill Bright, *The Holy Spirit: The Key to Supernatural Living,* Campus Crusade, 1980, 59.

In addition to studying God's Word, work with your group leader to create a plan for personal study, worship, and application between now and the next session. Select from the following optional activities to match your personal preferences and available time.

⬆ Worship

☑ Read your Bible. Complete the reading plan on page 72.

☐ Spend time with God by engaging the devotional experience on page 73.

☐ The Spirit empowers us to worship God in special ways. Take a moment to look up these central verses on how the Spirit empowers biblical, God-honoring worship: Ephesians 5:18-21; 6:18; 1 Corinthians 12:1-11; and Romans 5:5.

➡ ⬅ Personal Study

☐ Read and interact with "Who Is the Holy Spirit?" on page 74.

☐ Read and interact with "What Does the Holy Spirit Do?" on page 76.

⬅ ➡ Application

☐ At the end of your group time, you discussed how the Holy Spirit is leading you to action. If you don't yet know how the Holy Spirit is leading you, spend time in prayer for the Spirit to reveal to you what actions He wants you to take. Then ask Him for boldness as you follow His lead.

☐ Memorize Galatians 5:16: "I say then, walk by the Spirit and you will not carry out the desire of the flesh."

☐ Journal about your life in regard to the Spirit. Galatians 5 describes the life that is under the control of the Spirit. Take time to read Galatians 5:22-23. Identify the character qualities that the Spirit produces in a person's life. Then journal a prayer for the areas you would like to see more of in your own life.

☐ Other:

 # WORSHIP

READING PLAN

Read through the following Scripture passages this week. Use the space provided to record your thoughts and responses.

Day 1
John 16:7-15

Day 2
Acts 1:1-8

Day 3
John 14:25-31

Day 4
Romans 8:26-28

Day 5
Isaiah 11:2

Day 6
John 14:12-17

Day 7
Ezekiel 36:25-28

JESUS AND THE HOLY SPIRIT

Jesus' power was always attributed to the power of the Spirit. Look at some of the following examples from the New Testament:

- The Spirit was involved in the birth of Christ. According to Matthew 1:18, before Mary and Joseph were married, she was found to be pregnant by the Holy Spirit.
- In another account, an angel appeared to Mary and declared that she would bear the Messiah. She said, "How can this be, since I have not been intimate with a man?" and the angel said, "The Holy Spirit will come upon you, and the power of the Most High will overshadow you. Therefore, the holy One to be born will be called the Son of God" (Luke 1:34-35).
- The Spirit was also involved in the growth and development of Jesus. In Luke 2:40, Jesus "grew up and became strong, filled with wisdom, and God's grace was on Him."
- At His baptism, Jesus was anointed by the Holy Spirit and launched His public ministry (see Matt. 3:13-17).
- Jesus was led by the Spirit into the wilderness to be tempted and came out empowered by the Spirit (see Luke 4:1-14).
- In His first sermon, Luke 4:18, He said, "The Spirit of the Lord is on Me."
- It was by the power of the Spirit that He drove out demons, taught the multitude, and gave Him joy in ministry.
- Hebrews 9:14 says that by the Spirit Jesus offered Himself up to God as a sacrifice, and Romans 8:11 says that by that same Spirit Jesus was raised from the dead.

From beginning to end, Jesus was led and empowered by the Holy Spirit. That was the secret to His ministry! While Jesus was fully God, He was also fully man. And the same power Jesus held—power that came directly from His dependence on the Holy Spirit—is available to you and me. The Spirit wants to move powerfully in your life, but your access to the Spirit's power is in direct relationship to your dependence on Him. Greater dependence on the Spirit, greater power. Little dependence, little power.

How are you experiencing the Spirit's power in your life today?

You can live just like Jesus. First John 2:6 says, "The one who says he remains in Him should walk just as He walked." You can walk as Jesus walked, live as He lived, serve as He served, and love as He loved. But you can't do that in your own strength. You can only do it as you rely every day on the power of God's Spirit in your life.

WHO IS THE HOLY SPIRIT?

The Holy Spirit is a Person. Long before Jesus came to earth, God's people were struggling. Worship was dry. Sins were weighing them down. There was little change in their lives. They were frustrated in the little progress they had made spiritually. God promised them that one day He would give them a new heart and a new Spirit to live within them. He spoke these words through the prophet Ezekiel:

> I will give you a new heart and put a new spirit within you; I will remove your heart of stone and give you a heart of flesh.
> **EZEKIEL 36:26**

This promise came true when Jesus sent the Holy Spirit to His disciples. Jesus knew that His disciples were going to be devastated after His crucifixion. He knew they would feel abandoned and alone, so He said He was going to send "another helper"—a Person just like Him who would be with them forever, meet their every need, and never leave them.

Just after Jesus' death and resurrection, He instructed His disciples to go back to Jerusalem and wait for the Spirit to come. Then, on the Jewish holiday called Pentecost, the Spirit began to move powerfully on them. They were filled with boldness to preach the gospel. More than 3,000 people were saved that day and the church began (see Acts 2). Ever since that day, God has been moving in the hearts of His people through the power of His Spirit.

How have you experienced frustration in your relationship with God?

What obstacles keep you from relying on the power of God's Spirit?

Jesus said the Spirit of God was our "Advocate" (John 14:26, NIV). Other translations use different terms, including "Counselor" and "Comforter" (KJV). The original Greek word literally means "someone to come alongside."

The Holy Spirit is the Person called to come alongside you. Probably the best translation is simply "Helper" (NASB). The Spirit will be with you forever and will meet your every need and never leave you, just like He was with the disciples.

The Holy Spirit is God. He is described in many ways throughout the Bible. In Genesis 1:2, He is called "the Spirit of God." In Isaiah 61:1,"The Spirit of the Lord GOD." In Zechariah 12:10, He is the "spirit of grace." David called Him the "Holy Spirit" in Psalm 51:11. In Matthew 10:20, Jesus called Him "the Spirit of your Father." In Romans 1:4, He is called the "Spirit of holiness." In Romans 8:9, He is the "Spirit of Christ." In Galatians 4:6, He is called the "Spirit of His Son." In 1 Peter 4:14, He is the "Spirit of glory." Hebrews 9:14 says He is "the eternal Spirit."

All throughout Scripture we see that the Holy Spirit is God. To follow the Spirit is to follow God. To know the Spirit is to know God. To listen to the Spirit is to listen to God. In fact, all throughout the Scripture, the Holy Spirit possesses the attributes of God:

He is eternal.

> And I will ask the Father, and He will give you another Counselor to be with you forever.
> **JOHN 14:16**

He is all-knowing.

> Now God has revealed these things to us by the Spirit, for the Spirit searches everything, even the depths of God.
> **1 CORINTHIANS 2:10**

He is all-powerful.

> So he answered me, "This is the word of the LORD to Zerubbabel: 'Not by strength or by might, but by My Spirit,' says the LORD of Hosts.
> **ZECHARIAH 4:6**

He is ever-present.

> Where can I go to escape Your Spirit? Where can I flee from Your presence?
> **PSALM 139:7**

What else have you learned about the Spirit from your study of Scripture?

➡ ⬅ PERSONAL STUDY 2

WHAT DOES THE HOLY SPIRIT DO?

The Spirit's work in salvation: The Spirit of God is actively at work when we come to saving faith in Jesus. He convicts us of our sin, points us to Christ, and reveals the truth of Jesus. He also, at the point of our salvation, enables us to call on Jesus to be saved. He washes us, cleans us, makes us a part of God's family, and eternally secures us in Jesus forever! When we choose to follow Jesus, the Spirit indwells us and is with us forever. Just think about it.

You will never be left alone. You will never be apart from God. You will never be separated from God's Spirit.

Let's dig into God's Word and find out what the Spirit does to bring us to salvation. Answer the following questions according to the attached passage.

What does Jesus say the Spirit reveals to us (John 16:13)?

What does the Spirit bring into our hearts (John 16:8)?

What does the Spirit enable you to do (1 Cor. 12:1-11)?

What does the Spirit do for you (Titus 3:5-7)?

How does the Spirit secure you (Eph. 1:13-14)?

Where does the Spirit dwell (1 Cor. 6:19-20)?

The Spirit's work in transformation: From the moment of your spiritual birth, you enter into a new relationship with God, and this new relationship is accomplished by the Holy Spirit. He is the one who convicts you, draws you in, gives you new life, and places you into God's family. But He's also the One who transforms you. Look at some of the following ways the Spirit works after salvation.

The Spirit of God changes you.

Read Romans 8:5-8. What are some evidences that the Spirit of God is in control in your life?

The Spirit of God leads you.

Read Romans 8:12-17. Through what specific circumstances have you seen the Spirit lead you?

The Spirit of God empowers you.

Read Acts 1:8 and 1 Corinthians 12:4-7. In what areas do you feel inadequate to be used by God?

How do these passages encourage you in that you are empowered by the Spirit?

He is the one who convicts you, draws you in, gives you new life, and places you into God's family. He is also the one who changes you from the inside out, making you more and more like Jesus. He leads you in daily decisions, He guides you in wisdom, He convicts and changes parts of your character, and He produces new desires for God and for good. He also fills you with joy, peace, love, kindness, faithfulness, goodness, patience, gentleness, and self-control. It's the Spirit that empowers you to serve God, love others and share what Jesus has done for you! You cannot accomplish this on your own; it's a work of the Spirit. And the joyful Christian life is a life lived walking in step with the Spirit.

THE DOCTRINE OF THE CHURCH

God's people gather for community
and scatter for a cause.

REFLECT

In the previous session we learned about the Person and the power of the Holy Spirit. The Spirit is active in our salvation and also in our personal transformation. We also learned that the Spirit moved powerfully in the early church, empowering them to boldly preach about Jesus and make disciples.

We'll conclude this resource by taking a closer look at the church. First, take a moment to talk as a group about your recent experiences.

Which of the assignments did you explore this week? How did it go?

What did you learn or experience while reading the Bible?

What questions would you like to ask?

PRAY

Begin the session by connecting with God through prayer. Use the following guidelines as you connect with Him:

- Pray for God's Spirit to move in your time today.

- Pray for your hearts and minds to be open to what God is doing through His church.

- Ask for wisdom as you study what it means to join the church in working to achieve Christ's mission.

INTRODUCTION

Picture the following scenes:

- A small group meets in secret, quietly huddling in a subdued living room. Their presence isn't legal in Saudi Arabia. If they're caught, some could be sent to prison, others could lose their lives. The room falls silent as they hear footsteps outside the door.

- Thousands of affluent suburbanites gather in a large, state-of-the-art building in Atlanta. The lights, video, and production represent the best of the best. People come dressed in casual clothes, carrying their coffee into the worship center. The band cranks up and the room is flooded with moving lights and haze. The people begin to worship with their hands and voices raised.

- Everyone wears white jumpsuits. Guards are posted around the room. As men file in, smiles break across their faces. A band begins to play upbeat music, which fills the hopeless space with joy. The men clap their hands in celebration. A man comes to the microphone and declares: "Brothers, we once were free on the outside. Now we may be in prison, but we are free on the inside!"

- An organ plays as robed choir members sway back and forth to the music. Even though they are few, they make a joyful noise. The people are sitting in old pews, meeting behind stained-glass windows that picture the life of Jesus. The pastor gets up to proclaim hope to his congregation. Outside, the drug dealers and gangs make inner city Detroit a fearful place to live.

- Only one light bulb illuminates the cinder-block building. People rode in the back of pickup trucks for several miles to get there, traversing the jungles of Guatemala. Most hadn't eaten all day, but after the service is over they will share tortillas and soft drinks. Someone stands with a guitar and begins to lead out in song.

What do all these scenes have in common?

What comes to mind when you hear the word "church"?

KNOW THE STORY

The early church was a powerful movement that was both initiated and sustained by God. People were saved. Lives were transformed. The gospel was preached, and people were sent out to tell the nations about Jesus.

Yet even in the early church, there were times when Christians needed a reminder to continue meeting and fulfilling their purpose.

In this passage below, the author of Hebrews reminded his fellow Christians about the wonderful access they have to God because of Jesus. He encouraged them to continue gathering together as a church to fulfill their mission.

[19] Therefore, brothers, since we have boldness to enter the sanctuary through the blood of Jesus, [20] by a new and living way He has opened for us through the curtain (that is, His flesh), [21] and since we have a great high priest over the house of God, [22] let us draw near with a true heart in full assurance of faith, our hearts sprinkled clean from an evil conscience and our bodies washed in pure water. [23] Let us hold on to the confession of our hope without wavering, for He who promised is faithful. [24] And let us be concerned about one another in order to promote love and good works, [25] not staying away from our worship meetings, as some habitually do, but encouraging each other, and all the more as you see the day drawing near.
HEBREWS 10:19-25

What are your initial reactions to this passage?

On a practical level, what does it mean to "be concerned about one another in order to promote love and good works"?

As we continue exploring the doctrine of the church, we'll see how this passage not only guides us in understanding what the church is, but also how we should live and work as members of that institution.

UNPACK THE STORY

WHAT IS THE CHURCH?

The church is a family. The church isn't an organization, a business, or an entrepreneurial enterprise. When a person comes to faith in Jesus, he or she becomes part of God's family—the church. Just as someone is born into their physical family, Jesus said you must be "born again" (John 3:3) to get into God's family. In God's family, God is our "Father" (Gal. 4:6), Jesus is our big brother (see Heb. 2:11), and Christians become brothers and sisters (see 1 Cor. 7:15) as members of God's household (see Gal. 6:10).

Earthly families grow when children leave home to start their own families. You don't stop being a member of your family when you leave home, but you do gain the opportunity to expand that family by starting something new. The same is true in the church.

How have you experienced the blessings of a church family?

In God's family, God is our Father, Jesus is our big brother, and Christians become brothers and sisters as members of God's household.

The scenarios you read in the introduction were all diverse pictures of local churches meeting in different places, cultures, and environments. Such meetings are vital for every follower of Christ. It's not enough to be a part of God's family on a grand scale—what we refer to as the "universal church." We also need to be connected to a local collection of disciples.

In other words, God wants you to find a home in a local church family. Scripture confirms this truth. The majority of instruction in the Bible concerning the church has in mind a local congregation of believers. In fact, it would be a foreign concept to the biblical authors to think about being in the universal church without attending a local church.

So, what is the church? Here's one of many possible definitions: *The church is a family of baptized believers in Jesus Christ who gather for community and scatter for the cause of telling the world about Jesus.*

What are the consequences of avoiding membership in a local church?

What would you add to the above definition of "the church"?

GATHER FOR COMMUNITY AND SCATTER FOR A CAUSE

Now that we have a basic definition of the church, let's look at what it means to gather for community and scatter for a cause.

First, God's people are called to be part of a community. The early church experienced community in a way that created inseparable and unbreakable bonds. God worked in powerful ways. The apostles taught, lives were changed, and the Spirit moved. People generously gave to meet one another's needs. They spent their time eating together in their homes and gathering in the temple courts for worship.

It was an incredible period for the church.

Read Acts 2:41-47. What do you find most appealing in these verses? Why?

What obstacles prevent modern churches from experiencing that level of community?

The church isn't only called to gather for community, but also to scatter for a cause. As disciples of Jesus Christ, we are called to make disciples of Jesus Christ—who make disciples, who make more disciples, and so on. That was one of Jesus' final commands.

> ¹⁹ Go, therefore, and make disciples of all nations, baptizing them in the name of the Father and of the Son and of the Holy Spirit, ²⁰ teaching them to observe everything I have commanded you. And remember, I am with you always, to the end of the age."
> **MATTHEW 28:19-20**

God's people are called to be part of a community. The early church experienced community in a way that created inseparable and unbreakable bonds. God worked in powerful ways.

How does the church make it easier for you to spread the gospel in your community?

What hinders the church from having a greater influence in modern culture?

ENGAGE

We've learned that the church has two primary functions: (1) to gather for community, and (2) to scatter with a cause. It's easy to look at the church described in the Bible and desire to be in a church like that. It seems so perfect, without any problems or challenges. But even the early church was imperfect. They dealt with conflict, baggage from the past, power plays, immorality, and bad leadership. But through it all, people loved Jesus and worked hard to correct the problems and be a true reflection of Jesus to the world.

Today, there are no perfect churches. Churches are filled with and led by imperfect people. And just as there are no perfect families, there are some families that are healthy because they work through conflict, exercise grace and forgiveness, and work together for a common goal. The same is true of the church. When people in churches work through their conflict in the proper way, treat each other with grace and forgiveness, and work together for the sake of the gospel, they find health and peace.

Take a moment to share your church experience in your group.

How can a church practically work through conflict, exercise grace and forgiveness, and work together for a common goal?

PRAYER REQUESTS

....

....

....

....

....

....

....

....

....

In addition to studying God's Word, work with your group leader to create a plan for personal study, worship, and application between now and the next session. Select from the following optional activities to match your personal preferences and available time.

⬆ Worship

☑ Read your Bible. Complete the reading plan on page 86.

☐ Spend time with God by engaging the devotional experience on page 87.

☐ One unique trait of the church is that it gathers to worship Jesus. Sometimes that worship takes place through music, the Lord's Supper, baptism, the reading and teaching of God's Word, giving, and serving. How is the gospel clearly seen as the church worships in each of these ways? Take time this week to worship God with other believers in a local church.

➡ ⬅ Personal Study

☐ Read and interact with "God's People Gather for Community" on page 88.

☐ Read and interact with "God's People Scatter for a Cause" on page 90.

⬅ ➡ Application

☐ Read Hebrews 13:7,17. According to these verses, how should you respond to leaders who seek to lead the church to fulfill the mission of making disciples? Send an email this week to a pastor or church leader who has influenced you the most. Thank them for their example, their faithfulness to teach God's Word, and their investment in your life.

☐ Memorize Hebrews 10:25 (NLT): "Let us not neglect our meeting together, as some people do, but encourage one another, especially now that the day of his return is drawing near."

☐ Journal your church experience. Take some time to get alone with God and reflect on your church experience. You may have had a wonderful church experience or perhaps one that has been hurtful or disappointing. Write down your reflections in a letter to God. Ask Him to remove any pain inflicted by people in the church and to replace it with a love for His church.

☐ Other:

 **WORSHIP**

READING PLAN

Read through the following Scripture passages this week. Use the space provided to record your thoughts and responses.

Day 1
Colossians 3:12-17

Day 2
Acts 2:37-47

Day 3
Ephesians 2:13-22

Day 4
Romans 12:4-8

Day 5
Ephesians 4:1-16

Day 6
1 Corinthians 16:10-24

Day 7
Romans 16:17-20

THE BRIDE OF CHRIST

Jesus loves His church. In fact, the church is called the "bride of Christ." In Ephesians 5:25-27, the apostle Paul describes the kind of love Jesus has for His church. He said that Jesus loved the church so much that He "gave Himself for her." This is a reference to the cross. Jesus loved His church and His people so much that He was willing to endure whatever sacrifice, pay whatever price needed to restore them back to fellowship with Him.

Picture how much a young groom loves his bride. He watches her walk down the aisle, her white dress trailing behind her, her face aglow with love for her husband. The ring of his affection glistens from her finger, a symbol of his covenant love for her. He has chosen her. He has sacrificed for her. He is committed to protecting, leading, and loving her for the rest of his life. He has a home prepared for her, and soon he will gather her in his arms and carry her across that threshold, and his love for her will never die. That is a picture of how Jesus feels about you—His church, His bride. Jesus has set His affection and love on you. He has bought you with His own blood through His sacrifice on the cross (see 1 Pet. 1:18-19). He has made a covenant, an eternal promise that He will never break (see Matt. 26:28). He has made you clean, washing away your sin and making you right with Him (see 1 John 1:9), and one day He is coming to get you.

Revelation 19:6-7 describes the end of time. Jesus will come for His bride! He will gather His church up in His arms and take us to His Father's house in heaven where we will be with Him forever (see John 14:2-3). That's how much Jesus loves His church. That's how much Jesus loves you.

What emotions do you experience when you think about Christ's love for the church? What stands out to you most about His love for us?

Paul says Jesus also loved the church enough to purify and clean up His church. When you become a part of God's family, Jesus not only restores you back to Himself, but He cleans you up, inside and out. All the old life, the old mistakes, the old baggage is gone and you are pure and clean in His eyes. Jesus also loves His church so much that He promises to never leave His church. God has no orphans. He never leaves His people. He will never forsake you. You are His forever.

GOD'S PEOPLE GATHER FOR COMMUNITY

The church is a group of believers who gather to experience biblical community. Acts 2:42-47 gives us a great snapshot of what this biblical community looks like.

> [42] And they devoted themselves to the apostles' teaching, to the fellowship, to the breaking of bread, and to the prayers. [43] Then fear came over everyone, and many wonders and signs were being performed through the apostles. [44] Now all the believers were together and held all things in common. [45] They sold their possessions and property and distributed the proceeds to all, as anyone had a need. [46] Every day they devoted themselves to meeting together in the temple complex, and broke bread from house to house. They ate their food with a joyful and humble attitude, [47] praising God and having favor with all the people. And every day the Lord added to them those who were being saved.
> ACTS 2:42-47

Let's look at the four key elements of biblical community given to us in verse 42.

The church devoted themselves to the apostle's teaching. One key element of a biblical church is devotion to the preaching and teaching of God's Word. This was the very thing Paul was referring to when he said, "And now I commit you to God and to the message of His grace, which is able to build you up and to give you an inheritance among all who are sanctified" (Acts 20:32).

How have you seen growth in the church because of a commitment to the teaching and preaching of God's Word?

What does Paul mean when he says a commitment to the Word will "build you up and give you an inheritance among all who are sanctified"?

The church devoted themselves to fellowship. Not only were they devoted to God's Word, they were devoted to each other. The word *fellowship* means to be partners together. It means to share life together. Far from just coming to church and quickly leaving, fellowship means spending time caring for each other and partnering together in the gospel.

What would you consider genuine Christian fellowship?

The church devoted themselves to breaking bread. Some interpret this to mean simply sharing meals together, and the early church certainly did that. Acts 2:46 says, "breaking bread in their homes, they received their food with glad and generous hearts" (ESV). But the breaking of bread in Acts 2:42 could also refer to the Lord's Supper, a special meal observed by Christ followers to remember the death, burial and resurrection of Jesus.

Why is it important for believers to be reminded of the gospel of Christ by partaking in the Lord's Supper together?

What are other ways the church can be intentional about reminding each other of Christ's sacrifice on the cross?

The church devoted themselves to prayers. The early church was a praying church. There are times when we need to pray alone (see Matt. 6:6), but there are also times when it's important for the church to gather together and pray for each other.

Which of these elements of biblical community is carried out best in your church? What makes it so effective?

How can you contribute to one of these elements in the life of your church?

GOD'S PEOPLE SCATTER FOR A CAUSE

The early church took Jesus' mandate to tell the world seriously. Within two years, they had "filled Jerusalem" with the gospel (Acts 5:28). Within five years there were multiple churches (Acts 9:30). In 19 years, they had "turned the world upside down" (Acts 17:6), and within 28 years, the gospel had spread all over the known world (see Col. 1:5-6).

Which is most impressive to you?

Why do you think the early church had so much success with the spreading of the gospel?

The early church took Jesus' mandate in the Great Commission seriously, and the church today still takes seriously the Great Commission to tell the world the hope we have in Jesus. That is why men and women, college students, families, vocational missionaries, and volunteer workers go all around the world to declare the good news of the gospel.

Sharing with people the message of life is the job of the church. We are "ambassadors for Christ" (2 Cor. 5:20-21). Just as an ambassador lives in a foreign land, we are strangers and foreigners in this world, and our citizenship is in heaven. While we live in this world, we reflect Christ to people who don't know Him, and we tell people the good news about Jesus. Telling people about Jesus is a huge privilege for the church, but it's also an awesome responsibility.

Who shared the gospel with you for the first time?

Why do you think it's important for the church to be actively sharing the gospel?

The apostle Paul said he was "obligated" to take the gospel to every kind of people (see Rom. 1:14). He boldly proclaimed the gospel because it is "God's power for salvation to everyone who believes" (Rom. 1:16). God still changes people's lives today when they hear the gospel and believe on Jesus for their salvation. Paul also wrote this in 2 Timothy:

> And what you have heard from me in the presence of many witnesses, commit to faithful men who will be able to teach others also.
> **2 TIMOTHY 2:2**

What was Paul telling Timothy in this passage? How is this applicable for us today?

Read the following passage, and record how each speak to the spreading of the gospel. Then comment on how we can apply each to our own ministry to the world.

1 Thessalonians 1:6-8

1 Timothy 2:3-4

Revelation 7:9

What are practical ways churches can do a better job at scattering for a cause? Give several examples.

DISCIPLESPATH

If your group is continuing on the *Disciples Path* journey, choose your next study using the chart below or find other discipleship studies at *www.lifeway.com/goadults*

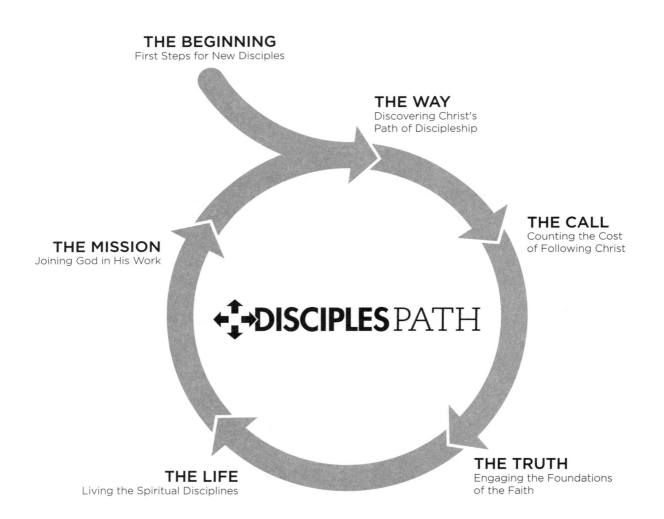

THE BEGINNING
First Steps for New Disciples

THE WAY
Discovering Christ's
Path of Discipleship

THE CALL
Counting the Cost
of Following Christ

THE MISSION
Joining God in His Work

DISCIPLESPATH

THE TRUTH
Engaging the Foundations
of the Faith

THE LIFE
Living the Spiritual Disciplines

TAKE THE NEXT STEP.

Disciples Path is a series of resources founded on Jesus' model of discipleship. Created by experienced disciple makers across the nation, it is an intentional path of transformational discipleship. While most small-group studies facilitate transformation through relationship and information, these disciple-making resources do it through the principles of modeling, practicing, and multiplying.

- Leaders model a biblical life.
- Disciples follow and practice from the leader.
- Disciples become disciple makers and multiply through *Disciples Path*.

Each of the six studies in the *Disciples Path* series has been written and approved by disciple makers for one-on-one settings as well as small groups. The series includes:

1. THE BEGINNING
Take the first step for a new believer and new disciple.

2. THE WAY
Walk through the Gospels and follow the journey of Jesus and the first disciples.

3. THE CALL
Gain a deeper understanding of what it means to follow Christ in everyday life.

4. THE TRUTH
Dive into the doctrinal truths of biblical discipleship.

5. THE LIFE
Take a deeper look at the essential disciplines and practices of following Christ.

6. THE MISSION
Get equipped for God's mission and discover your role in joining Him in the world.

To learn more or take the next step, visit *lifeway.com/disciplespath*

LEADER INSTRUCTIONS

As a group leader or mentor, you have a vital role in the process of discipleship—one that involves both blessing and responsibility. Keep in mind the following guidelines as you faithfully obey the Great Commission.

YOUR GOAL

Remember that your ultimate goal in the discipleship process is spiritual transformation. The best fruit for your efforts as a leader is spiritual growth that results in transformed hearts—both for you and for the disciples under your care.

Remember also that spiritual transformation is most likely to occur when a godly leader applies truth to the heart of a person while that person is in a teachable posture. As the leader, you have direct control over the first two of those conditions; you can also encourage and support disciples as they seek a teachable posture. Take advantage of those opportunities.

YOUR METHODS

Use the following suggestions as you work toward the goal of spiritual transformation.

- **Pray daily.** Studies have shown that leaders who pray every day for the disciples under their care see the most spiritual fruit during the discipleship process. Your ultimate goal is spiritual transformation; therefore, seek the Holy Spirit.

- **Teach information.** This resource contains helpful information on the basic elements of the Christian faith. During group discussions, you'll want to be familiar enough with the content to avoid reading each page verbatim. Highlighting key words or even creating your own bullet points will help you facilitate the time most effectively. Prepare in advance.

- **Seek conversation.** As you lead disciples through the material, seek to engage them in meaningful conversation. To help you, discussion questions have been provided throughout the group portion of each session. These questions provide an opportunity to pause and allow each disciple to react to the teaching. They also allow you as the disciple-maker an opportunity to gauge how each person is progressing along the path of discipleship.

- **Model practices.** Many disciples learn best by observing others. Therefore, each session of this resource includes opportunities for you to model the attributes, disciplines, and practices of a growing disciple of Jesus. Take advantage of these opportunities by intentionally showing disciples how to pray, interact with God's Word, worship God, and so on—and by inviting feedback and questions.

May God bless your efforts to guide others toward the blessing of new life through Christ and continued transformation through His Spirit.

NOTES

DISCIPLES PATH
Group Directory

Name: _____

Home Phone: _____

Mobile Phone: _____

Email: _____

Social Media: _____

Name: _____

Home Phone: _____

Mobile Phone: _____

Email: _____

Social Media: _____

Name: _____

Home Phone: _____

Mobile Phone: _____

Email: _____

Social Media: _____

Name: _____

Home Phone: _____

Mobile Phone: _____

Email: _____

Social Media: _____

Name: _____

Home Phone: _____

Mobile Phone: _____

Email: _____

Social Media: _____

Name: _____

Home Phone: _____

Mobile Phone: _____

Email: _____

Social Media: _____

Name: _____

Home Phone: _____

Mobile Phone: _____

Email: _____

Social Media: _____

Name: _____

Home Phone: _____

Mobile Phone: _____

Email: _____

Social Media: _____

Name: _____

Home Phone: _____

Mobile Phone: _____

Email: _____

Social Media: _____

Name: _____

Home Phone: _____

Mobile Phone: _____

Email: _____

Social Media: _____